RISE ABOVE SERIES
4

ALPHA OMEGA
PARADIGM

Critical Connections

FOR

Every Christian

Reed D. Tibbetts

ALPHA OMEGA PARADIGM
© 2017 by Reed D. Tibbetts

Published by Insight International, Inc.
contact@freshword.com
www.freshword.com
918-493-1718

All Scripture quotations are taken from the *New American Standard Bible®*, © 1960, 1962, 1963, 1968, 1971, 1972, 1973, 1975, 1977, 1995 by The Lockman Foundation. Used by permission.www.Lockman.org

ISBN: 978-1-943361-26-7
E-book ISBN: 978-1-943361-27-4

Library of Congress Control Number: 2016958589

Printed in the United States of America.

ENDORSEMENTS FOR
ALPHA OMEGA PARADIGM

"I have known my friend, Reed Tibbetts, for thirty-six years. I am convinced that Reed is a man of absolute integrity. He is a diligent student of the Bible. He is comfortable in his relationship with the Holy Spirit. I am anticipating further Biblical teachings from Reed Tibbetts."

— Richard C. Benjamin Sr.,
Apostle and Founding Pastor of
Abbott Loop Christian Center,
Anchorage, Alaska

"Reed serves faithfully and loyally as one of the elders in the church I pastor. He is one of the best theological minds I have had the privilege of calling my friend. His teachings are a unique mix of potent ingredients that form a special recipe of the truth, and reach the minds and spirits of those he teaches. Relax, receive, and enjoy the concepts of his latest book."

— Mike Connaway, Senior Pastor of
VLife Church, McKinney, Texas
and Author of *My Third House*

"Reed Tibbetts is one of the most preeminent theologians I have ever met. He brings his steeped knowledge of the Bible, and uses his God-given anointing, to write books that encourage and challenge all believers to grow in their relationship with God. Reed has a great ability to reach all generations in his writings and teachings. He is truly a man of God."

— Gabriel Kvalvik, faithful member of
the *I Serve* team at VLife Church,
McKinney, Texas

DEDICATION

I dedicate this book, "Alpha Omega Paradigm" to my two granddaughters, Hannah and Alayah. At the time of this writing Hannah is twelve years old; Alayah is ten. My wife and I have had many precious times with the girls. We especially like traveling in our motor home with them. We have seen the Grand Canyon, visited Route 66 from Texas to California; celebrated family reunions in California and Oregon. We have handled alligators in Louisiana, marveled at Mt. Rushmore, yelled as a buffalo came down the road toward us in Yellowstone National Park. We've been 200 feet underground in the Jewel Cave, driven across Kansas and Nebraska and seen corn, corn and more corn. Everywhere we go, we try to visit unique local restaurants, and almost always we eat ice cream afterward. They love ice cream and so does Grandpa! And each time we are together we take special Scriptures to memorize. I take the Scripture opportunity to teach them and Grandma and Grandpa pour everything we can into our girls, so that they grow up to serve the Lord in great and mighty ways. The Alpha Omega Paradigm is all about Christians having the critical connections they need, in order to live strong lives for the Lord. Our granddaughters have accepted Jesus Christ as their Savior and Lord, and been baptized in the name of the Lord Jesus Christ. They have the cornerstone that they need: Jesus Christ. And they are being taught all the connections that will keep them solid and strong in the faith of the Lord and in the work of the ministry. Girls, I love you and I am proud of your Christianity. Keep the faith!

CONTENTS

Part Seven: Appropriating the Power of Almighty God

WHY THE RISE ABOVE SERIES?

Isaiah 2:2, 3 – The word which Isaiah the son of Amoz saw concerning Judah and Jerusalem. Now it will come about that in the last days the mountain of the house of the LORD will be established as the chief of the mountains, and will be raised above the hills; and all the nations will stream to it. And many peoples will come and say, "Come let us go up to the mountain of the LORD, to the house of the God of Jacob; that He may teach us concerning His ways and that we may walk in His paths." For the law will go forth from Zion and the word of the LORD from Jerusalem.

Micah 1:1; 4:1, 2 – The word of the LORD which came to Micah of Moresheth...And it will come about in the last days that the mountain of the house of the LORD will be established as the chief of the mountains. It will be raised above the hills, and the peoples will stream to it. Many nations will come and say, "Come and let us go up to the mountain of the LORD and to the house of the God of Jacob, that He may teach us about His ways and that we may walk in His paths." For from Zion will go forth the law, even the word of the LORD from Jerusalem.

Matthew 5:14-16 – You are the light of the world. A city set on a hill cannot be hidden; nor does anyone light a lamp and put it under a basket, but on the lampstand, and it gives light to all who are in the house. Let your light shine before men in such a way that they may see your good works, and glorify your Father who is in heaven.

Matthew 28:19, 20 – Go therefore and make disciples of all the nations, baptizing them in the name of the Father and the Son and the Holy Spirit, teaching them to observe all that I commanded you; and lo, I am with you always, even to the end of the age.

John 10:10 – The thief comes only to steal and kill and destroy; I came that they may have life, and have it abundantly.

All of these Scriptures are talking about the church of the Lord Jesus Christ in the last days, describing how people from all nations and people groups will come into the church. It is all about the end times ingathering of people into the kingdom of God and the church of our Lord.

Back in the eighth century B.C., during the reigns of the Kings Ahaz and Hezekiah in the nation of Judah, we had two very different scenarios of what happened to the house of God (the Jerusalem temple). It can be summed up very simply: King Ahaz closed the doors of the house of the LORD (II Chronicles 28:24); King Hezekiah opened the doors of the house of the LORD (II Chronicles 29:3). There were also two prophets (Isaiah and Micah) who spoke identical prophecies about the very last days. Isaiah came from an aristocratic family, while Micah was a peasant farmer: two very different classes, but an identical prophecy from the LORD. This end time prophecy, through shadow and substance, tells the end times church exactly how people will be attracted to and come into the church of the Lord Jesus Christ.

The mountain of the house of the LORD, the mountain of the LORD, the house of the God of Jacob, Zion and Jerusalem are all terms referring to the temple in Jerusalem, where God's presence resided. In the New Testament, the church is the temple of God, for His presence resides inside every person who has accepted Jesus Christ as Savior and Lord. This is what the Old Testament prophecy is saying to the church:

- In the last days the church of the Lord Jesus Christ will be raised above all other religions, philosophies and movements. As it is established as chief among all religions, many people from all nations and all kinds of people groups will come into the church, looking to learn the ways of the LORD and how to walk in His paths. Simply put, there will be a large group of people who will become Christians.

This is what I referred to earlier as the end times ingathering. We want this to happen, and it is clearly the will of God, for He is not willing for any to perish, but for all to come to repentance (II Peter 3:9). So how will the church rise above the hills, that is, the religions, philosophies and movements of the world? The answer is found in the teachings of Jesus during the Sermon on the Mount. The church becomes like a city set on a hill: it can't be hidden. The people in the church will be a light that shines out to all people. We are to shine in such a way that they see our good works and glorify God. Our good works are our very lives: our abundant lives. People will see the abundant lives that we live in Jesus, and come into the church to learn more; they will marvel at the ways of the LORD that give us abundant life, and accepting Christ, they will walk in the same abundant lives that we show them.

We have used many methods to shine forth our light and spread the gospel (T.V., internet, social media, evangelism crusades, door-to-door witnessing, street preaching, picketing, political involvement, etc.) and we spend millions of dollars on those methods. But are we seeing the end times ingathering, with masses of people coming into the church? Certainly not in the United States. So I ask another question: are we living the abundant life in Jesus Christ that shows itself as far superior to other religions, philosophies and life styles? Are the people of the world looking at the people in the church and saying, "Wow! Their lives are far superior to and way above anything we are seeing or experiencing. Let's go into the church of Jesus Christ and check it out!" The answer is no. On a one-to-one scale, there are some individuals who come into the church for this very reason, but not on the massive scale spoken of in the prophecies of Isaiah and Micah.

We, the church of Jesus Christ, need to focus our attention on living the successful, powerful, abundant life that God has for us. In every aspect of life: marriage, child-raising, work, business, finances, physical health, mental health, spiritual dimension, etc., we need to live our lives in such a way that it shines brightly and brings people into the church to check it out. Instead of settling for a so-so or struggling life, and making it to heaven by the skin of our teeth; or being content that we are moral and live stable prosperous lives, we need to live the abundant life that results in many coming into the church. So the books of the "Rise Above" series are all about Christians learning to walk in the abundant life. Rise above, and see the harvest of people coming into the church to learn the ways of the Lord and how to walk in them. Many people will come to Jesus Christ to have the abundant life!

Alpha Omega Paradigm is a book about changing your view of what a successful Christian needs in connections throughout his Christian walk, that will bring the result of a solid, abundant life. Enjoy it, learn and increase your abundant life. Rise above!

INTRODUCTION

Alpha – Alpha is the first letter of the Greek alphabet, and it came from the first letter of the Phoenician alphabet. The Greeks assigned it the numeric value of (1), and it can carry the meaning of the beginning or the first. It is sometimes used to refer to the first or most significant occurrence of something. It can also have a social meaning within the animal kingdom, or even human society: the top individual (like the male wolf that is the leader of the pack, the alpha male). Jesus Christ is our Alpha; our number one, the top individual in our lives. His existence in our lives is the single most significant thing. He is our Alpha: your Alpha and my Alpha.

Omega – Omega is the last letter of the Greek alphabet. The Greeks assigned it the numeric value of (800), and it can carry the meaning of the finish, completion or ending. Interestingly enough, it is used extensively in science and mathematics to mean a whole lot of different things: ohms, oxygen, omega constants, etc. Jesus Christ is our Omega, our huge complete number, the One who completes our life, and leads us to the finish and ending of everything. His existence in our lives brings completion to our being. He is our Omega: your Omega and my Omega.

Alpha and Omega – When the two letters were used in one phrase, it carried the meaning of something all encompassing and complete. You and I might say, "We've done everything, from A to Z," meaning we have done everything for a job, project or mission. Jesus Christ calls Himself our Alpha and Omega, our all encompassing purpose and vision in life; the One who brings total completion to our walk. He is our Alpha and Omega: your Alpha and Omega and my Alpha and Omega.

Paradigm – A paradigm is a distinct set of concepts or thought patterns, including the theories, methods and standards that are used to come up with precepts, patterns and truths. These concepts and patterns form a model, template or archetype. When one arrives at a particular paradigm it becomes a clear, unique template to use to move forward in one's life and walk.

I often look at Wikipedia to help me understand word definitions, and that has certainly helped me in writing this book. And so I invite you to move forward with me as we consider the Alpha Omega Paradigm that Jesus Christ has given to us as Christians. I will lay out each precept within the paradigm, and break it down into lines and points. It will be a blessing for all of us.

Legend. Finding the will of the Holy Spirit will be a constant concept throughout this book. In one corner of the bottom of a map or blue print, one can find a "legend" box. It defines certain symbols or measurements that apply to the document. Just as a map or set of blueprints will have a legend that fundamentally stays the same page after page, so we have a "legend" in the Alpha Omega Paradigm. The legend for every precept and line will be the same: always find the will of the Holy Spirit. His will is to do what the Father and the Son want; the will of the Father and the Son and the Holy Spirit is always the same. Hence the legend questions:

- What does the Holy Spirit want?

- What is the Holy Spirit doing?

- What is the Holy Spirit saying?

Part One

His Kingdom for a Paradigm!

(not My Kingdom for a Horse!)

Chapter One

REQUIRED: A PARADIGM SHIFT

Revelation 22:13 – I am the Alpha and the Omega, the first and the last, the beginning and the end.

I have been in full time ministry at many churches over the last 45 years, serving as a staff pastor in eight congregations, and as the senior pastor in three. I am presently one of the elders in a refreshing new congregation in McKinney, Texas, VLife Church, where I serve regularly with special prayer, prophetic gifts, and Bible teaching. Whatever my pastor requests that I do, I gladly do. Pastor Mike Connaway has a wonderful message of grace, hope and victory, and Sunday by Sunday, new people are becoming Christians. It has been thrilling to see so many embrace the Lord for the first time, or return to Him after having drifted away for a long time. In the midst of this enjoyable atmosphere, one of the other elders in our new congregation, Jon Lee, came to me after one Sunday morning service, with this simple observation: "Recently we have had a lot of new converts to the Lord, and we need to consider what to do in training and equipping them." It was a good point, and I began to consider what I could do to help. Now over the years I had developed many different courses and notebooks to teach new Christians: New Converts Class, Bible Foundations, New Additions Class, etc. I perused those materials, but felt no special prompting from the Holy Spirit, as to what to use. In fact, it seemed to me that while the teachings were true, they seemed to have a "hard works" approach to growing as a Christian.

As I considered this in prayer, the Lord impressed upon me this concept: "I am the Alpha and the Omega." I was aware that this language was used in Revelation, but hadn't really thought a lot about it over the years. So I looked at the three occurrences in Revelation, and found that the phrase was only spoken by Jesus. I decided to also look at other Scriptures that had the phrase; that's when I discovered that it was only used in Revelation. So the Alpha Omega concept that the Lord had impressed on me in prayer, was unique to the book of Revelation and to the Lord Himself! God was opening my mind to look at His teachings for new converts in a whole different way. He began to show me that there are precepts, crucial connections, that are absolutely necessary to the brand new Christian. But also, and this was really eye opening, these precepts, crucial connections, were absolutely necessary to the way-old Christian! So was born the concept of the Alpha Omega Paradigm.

Paradigm refers to a model, pattern, template, standard or archetype. The word was very much in vogue in the late 20th century, used frequently by business speakers and corporate coaches to point business leaders toward a new way of doing things. In order to succeed, people needed to make a "paradigm shift." They needed to let go of their past plans and patterns, and embrace a new template that would allow them to accomplish the mission. The problem was that managers didn't want to let go of the old way of doing things, because it had worked in the past, and they assumed it would work forever. Paradigm shift was very uncomfortable; it was major change, and we humans struggle with any kind of change.

I'm only right when I agree with Him!
Funny how that works, isn't it?

I have come to a point in my life where whatever God wants me to say or do, wherever He wants me to do it, and whenever He wants me to do it, I'm going to do. While I have struggled at times over the years in the work of the ministry to do what I wanted, He has humbled me to the point where I surrender to His way of doing things for His kingdom and His righteousness. For this reason, as He has shown me better paradigms I have shifted my paradigm as quickly as I can because He's always right, and I'm only right when I agree with Him! Funny how that works, isn't it? So I'm on board with Him about the Alpha Omega Paradigm. To state the paradigm simply: there are key connection precepts that are critical for very new Christians, for very old Christians, and for all Christians in between. These connection precepts are strong vertical and horizontal relationship lines that must be tended to and maintained throughout our Christian walk, and we never mature so much as Christians that we don't still need them. If they are neglected at any point along our Christian walk, we can stumble, stagger and even fall.

Since God was impressing the Alpha Omega Paradigm upon me, and it was going to require a paradigm shift, I had to ask myself: what's the present paradigm or practice that God wants to change? This has to do with the Christian walk and path; how a convert grows and matures. In the business world I found that almost everyone likes a good graph, especially one that shows growth going up and up and up! Picture in your mind what this kind of individual convert growth would look like on a graph. You would see the convert growth like a rising incline line on that graph: pretty straightforward. And as the convert grows, he doesn't need to keep doing the things he did at the beginning. He can put away the baby steps, and doesn't need to worry any longer about the ABC's of being a Christian. Once he has accepted a concept and does it, he doesn't need to hear it again, or worry about doing it anymore. So the graph line goes up and up and up! He tells himself that he doesn't need to lay again a foundation that he's already put in place. What very new Christians need, very old Christians don't need. Old Christians are above those beginning things, since they have traveled onward and upward on the rising incline line of Christian growth. That's the graph of the old paradigm. At least that's how our "old paradigm" eyes see it.

I am reminded of something that happened to me when I was pastoring a new church plant back in the 1980's. About once per year I would preach a sermon on financial giving – tithes and offerings. I always tried to put a new and refreshing spin on the Biblical principles of giving, so that the teaching would relate to new and old Christians. On this particular Sunday morning, when I announced the sermon topic, I had one man stand up and leave the service. I watched him walk out the front door. Now this man was my age, and was an elder-in-training who aspired to become an elder in our young congregation. After the service was over, I found myself outside the church front door and noticed this man sitting on the lawn about 100' away. I walked over and the ensuing conversation went something like this: Me: "I noticed you walk out of the service at the beginning of my message. Was anything wrong?" Him: I've already heard about tithing, and know about tithing, and I just didn't want to hear it again." Me: I do try to give different perspectives on our giving each time I teach on it. Was there something I said that bothered you, or is there something about the topic that you don't agree with? Him: No. I just don't need to hear it again. I'm beyond that, and I need something new, something with meat, to challenge me and interest me." Me: "We all need to be reminded of Biblical principles of conduct. I know I do." Him: "You need to preach and teach on topics that challenge me. I don't need milk anymore. I want meat!" I went on to correct and direct his thinking and conduct with regard to receiving teaching and consuming both milk and meat from the Word. This man was participating in weekly teaching sessions on the qualifications, conduct and ministry of an elder. I will add, sadly, that it was not long after that episode that he left the church, convinced that I didn't know how to pastor mature Christians. I cite this example to point out a common paradigm that older and very old Christians practice that needs to be interrupted, and replaced by the Alpha Omega Paradigm. While this old Christian growth paradigm looks like a rising incline line on a graph, the Alpha Omega Paradigm looks like a straight line on a graph that gets thicker and thicker the farther you go. And it seems to grow vertical lines down that also get thicker and thicker. It illustrates how the "Abiding in the Vine" principle just gets thicker and deeper day by day and year by year in our Christian walk. It is how we are supposed to mature as we grow. The graph line doesn't go gradually up and up and up. Rather it gets set at a high level (after all, all converts, new and old, are the righteousness of God in Christ Jesus). Rather than rising, it stays at the same high level, just getting thicker and thicker over the years. That's the graph of the new paradigm, the Alpha Omega Paradigm.

So, if a paradigm shift is required, why do humans in general, and Christians in particular, resist the needed paradigm shift?

1. We don't like interruptions. We want things to go on continuously. Paradigm shift involves stopping one plan, and starting another one, and that's interruption.

2. Common sense resists change. Since the things we are doing have worked in the past, our common sense says to keep on doing them. But our common sense often is at odds with God's pattern. His thoughts are far above our thoughts and His ways are far beyond our ways.

3. We don't want to make social adjustments or changes. We get used to our patterns and develop our social relationships around them. How we relate to everyone around us becomes part of the template of our actions. If we are required to make a shift in the paradigm, we resist it because we are comfortable with our relationships and don't want to change how they work.

Clinging to our social relationship patterns will keep us from the perfect plan of God. Grasping our own common sense will block us from the wisdom of His higher ways. And disliking interruptions will only keep us from experiencing God's fuller ways. We want all that God has for us; more importantly, we want to do all that God wants us to do!

Chapter Two

REJECTING THE ALPHA OMEGA PARADIGM

Christians can use a lot of excuses to avoid embracing the precepts of the Alpha Omega paradigm. Let's look at what I call paradigm rejecters, dismissers and "slide-offers."

From the new Christian:

1. This is too hard...I can't do this.

   What happens in this scenario is that the new Christian rejoices in the forgiving grace of Jesus, but like any human being, will resist the change of dehabituation – rehabituation that is part and parcel of the Christian walk. For example, they have always ruled their own life, but now Jesus is inside of them and wants to sit on the throne of their heart and yes, rule. That can represent some 180 degree changes. Another example: attending church regularly and doing something with the church people means that time that may have been used for leisure or slumber now is taken up doing "churchy" things. The point is that we have been pre-conditioned to believe change is hard. God is all about convincing, change and transformation, and that is really good for us. Satan is all about condemning, status quo and stagnation, and that is really bad for us.

Revelation 1:8 – "I am the Alpha and the Omega," says the Lord God, "who is and who was and who is to come, the Almighty."

Jesus is the Almighty, and He has the power to transform you and help you change. The reality is that all of the precepts of the Alpha Omega Paradigm are easy. God made it simple, so each Christian could either choose, or choose not to connect and maintain the connections of the Alpha and the Omega. New converts: don't let this excuse derail your Christian path.

2. I don't need this. Being saved is enough. By faith I have accepted the grace of Jesus and I know I have eternal life. You have told me that nothing I do can save me, but that Jesus died on the cross so that I could be saved, by grace through faith. Now you're telling me about things I need to do. I'm just going to stay the same and make it to heaven when I die.

   That is accurate and true. But there's even more blessing that we can have. I like to say it this way. Jesus came and died on the cross to give us eternal life and abundant life. The salvation of the cross is all about eternal life. But once we are set free from the precept (law) of sin and death by the cross, we can then walk in the abundant life that Jesus wants for us. Don't settle for less than your inheritance in Christ Jesus!

From the old Christian:

1. I don't need to repeat the ABC's. These precepts are simply ABC's, and I don't need to lay again an "elementary principles" foundation. I no longer have need of milk, but now eat the meat of the Word. That's

what Christian maturity is all about, and I am now a mature Christian.

Hebrews 6:1, 2 — Therefore leaving the elementary teaching about the Christ, let us press on to maturity, not laying again a foundation of repentance from dead works and of faith toward God, of instruction about washings, and laying on of hands, and the resurrection of the dead, and eternal judgment.

There are some initial principles and truths in our Christian walk that need to be cemented into the first steps on our Christian path: baptism, faith, eternal judgment, etc. If we keep constantly repenting, if we keep doubting whether we have faith, if we beg God to be washed again and again, we diminish the encompassing and complete propitiation of the work of Jesus on the cross for us; we look like bawling, squalling babies, rolling around in our wet, messy diapers, instead of taking our first toddling steps on the path that Jesus has for us. We need to walk, not roll around and bawl and squall. But the precepts of the Alpha Omega Paradigm are not initial ABC's. They are A to Z's, simple and essential connections that must be made and maintained throughout our Christian walk. Don't reject these crucial connections; embrace them and live abundantly!

2. I can do it on my own. I'm a grown up believer. I can do stuff without relying on others. There comes a time in every believer's life when they need to stand on their own two feet and do the really great things for God. Independent action and conduct is a sign of maturity in a Christian.

Philippians 4:13 — I can do all things through Him who strengthens me.

I Corinthians 12:21 – And the eye cannot say to the hand, "I have no need of you"; or again the head to the feet, "I have no need of you."

Real Christian maturity is evidenced by the realization and practice of being dependent upon God and His people. We are totally dependent upon Jesus at all times throughout our Christian walk, and interdependent upon our fellow Christian brothers and sisters, within the church, throughout the steps we take on our Christian path. That kind of real Christian maturity is expressed in the precepts we will establish in the Alpha Omega Paradigm. These connections are simple, accurate and consistent. Don't dismiss them quickly or lightly; they will bring clarity and consistency to your Christian walk.

3. I'm doing O.K. with what I am doing now. I don't need to change.

"The old is good enough."

Luke 5:39 – And no one, after drinking old wine wishes for new; for he says, "The old is good enough."

Christ was pointing out how uncomfortable we can be with change, and also how we can be content with how things are, and settle for less. I consume a lot of diet soda, and my favorite for almost 40 years has been diet Coke; not diet Pepsi, not diet RC, not diet X-brand cola. A while back Coca Cola put out a new diet cola drink called "Coke Zero." Just like diet Coke, it was cola with zero calories. Supposedly it tasted more like regular Coca Cola. Well, I was not interested in this new diet cola drink at all. I was content with diet Coke; I was used to the taste, it was diet and cola, and it was good enough for me. Well, one day I had an opportunity to get a half dozen 2-liter bottles of Coke Zero for free! If you know me, you know that I do not pass up an opportunity to get something for free. So I had to drink a different diet cola for a few days. And guess what? It tasted great, definitely reminding me of how the Coke I used to drink as a teenager tasted. To me, it tasted better than regular diet Coke! Imagine that! As you consider the precepts of the Alpha Omega Paradigm, don't let them slide off your back and out of your mind and life. Instead, taste and see that these principles will cement your strong Christian walk, and make you an even more effective worker in God's kingdom.

4. I don't want to interrupt my progress by changing how I look at things.

   Consider the quick answer that I have heard from so many trainers and teachers over the years: The wood-cutter, who pauses in his chopping to sharpen his axe, makes his work easier and increases his productivity. And so it is as we move along this Christian path; Christ, the Alpha Omega, equips us with great connections, and expects us to sharpen those connections as we walk the Christian walk.

5. I'm mature, and I don't want to look like a baby Christian. If I do things that brand new Christians also do, I will look like a baby Christian instead of a mature person of God. I've lived the Christian life for

years so that others will see me as a mature Christian, and I don't want to give that up. I am concerned about how others see me.

While we don't often admit it, we are very conscious of how people see us. We are concerned about the social cost of anything we might do. How will I look to other people? That comes from our pride. But embracing these Alpha Omega connections won't weaken your Christian walk, and not maintaining the connections could result in our stumbling, staggering or even falling as we walk the Christian path. And if that happens how will we look to other people then?

I have tried to address objections <u>before</u> we go through all of these wonderful Alpha Omega connections, so that we all can embrace these truths, and not be distracted or side tracked from what the Alpha and Omega (Jesus Christ) wants to teach us. His teachings are pure and clear, and I do not want to complicate them or obscure the simple truth. So I have made it my goal in the presentation of the Alpha Omega paradigm to make sure that the precepts are simple, accurate, broad, consistent and fruitful. By doing that I hope the required paradigm shift will be as easy for you as it has been for me.

Chapter Three

THE CORNERSTONE OF THE ALPHA OMEGA PARADIGM

Revelation 21:6 – Then He said to me, "It is done. I am the Alpha and the Omega, the beginning and the end. I will give to the one who thirsts from the spring of the water of life without cost."

I looked at every word and every phrase in the three Alpha Omega verses in Revelation. In Revelation 21:6 I saw phrases that obviously referred to the gospel of salvation: "It is done," reminded me of Christ's final words from the cross: "It is finished." To me both phrases refer to the completed work of salvation by grace through faith that Jesus accomplished for us by dying on the cross and paying the penalty for our sins. The phrase "I will give to the one who thirsts from the spring of the water of life without cost," also reminded me of the salvation conversation Jesus had with the Samaritan woman at the well:

John 4:10 – Jesus answered and said to her, "If you knew the gift of God, and who it is who said to you, 'Give me a drink,' you would have asked Him, and He would have given you living water."

The water of life and living water both refer to what Jesus Christ can give to any and every human who chooses to accept

Him by faith and thus drink of eternal life. The simple, clear base for the Alpha Omega Paradigm is the same one for everything in the Christian life: We must be born again. Before any connection precepts can work in our lives, we must receive Jesus Christ as our Savior and Lord.

Acts 4:11, 12 – He is the stone which was rejected by you, the builders, but which became the chief corner stone. And there is salvation in no one else; for there is no other name under heaven that has been given among men by which we must be saved.

In New Testament times the cornerstone was the principal stone placed at the corner of an edifice. It was the first stone placed in the construction process, and all other stones were set in reference to this cornerstone. So the placing of every stone was measured from this stone, and the position of the entire structure was based upon the cornerstone. If measurements from the cornerstone were not taken, the other corners would not be square, and it obviously follows that the whole building would be put out of square. Everything had to be measured from and against the placement of the cornerstone.

I have seen people build their Christian lives on certain charismatic individuals, but that has not worked. When the charismatic person stumbled or fell, those people also stumbled and fell. They had the wrong cornerstone.

I have seen people build their Christian walk on certain dynamic movements, but that has not worked. In the 20th century there were many significant movements: the Pentecostal movement, the Holiness movement, the Latter Rain movement, the Jesus People movement, the Charismatic movement, the Apostolic movement. All represented great truths, but were not in and of themselves the needed cornerstone. Movements come and go, and when that particular movement faded away, these people also faded away from the Christian walk. They had the wrong cornerstone.

I have seen people build their Christian lives on certain energetic organizations, but that has not worked. Maybe it was a particular denomination, or a political grouping (such as the Moral Majority), or a particular ministry emphasis (such as Basic Youth Conflicts). All were great efforts and had very good effects as they progressed, but emphasis and ministry change through the years, as they should, and so some organizations changed, while others died. So too, some of these people who didn't change with what the Holy Spirit was doing, died away, or became empty shells, like the walking dead. They had the wrong cornerstone.

The cornerstone upon which the Alpha Omega Paradigm is based is Jesus Christ and His gospel.

Every paradigm, principle and precept in the kingdom of God must be built upon the abiding Son of God and the salvation gospel that He gave us on the cross. The cornerstone upon which the Alpha Omega Paradigm is based is Jesus Christ and His gospel. As the old hymn said, "My hope is built on nothing less than Jesus' blood and righteousness."

When Jesus Christ died on the cross, one of the last things He said before He gave up His spirit and died was the simple phrase, "It is finished." Certainly His physical life on this earth was finished. But it meant so much more. He came to earth to die on the cross for the world's salvation. God's mighty work of redemption was completed at His death.

II Corinthians 5:21 – He made Him who knew no sin to be sin on our behalf, so that we might become the righteousness of God in Him.

In Revelation 21, the Alpha Omega passage begins and ends with the cornerstone of everything Christian. When He said, "It is done," it clearly reminds us of what He said on the cross, "It is finished." And the concluding promise of the verse is all about being born again. "I will give to the one who thirsts from the spring of the water of life without cost." As I mentioned before, the spring of the water of life reminds us of what Jesus said to the woman at the well in Samaria:

John 4:14 – but whoever drinks of the water that I will give him shall never thirst; but the water that I will give him will become in him a well of water springing up to eternal life."

The gift of eternal life from Jesus is without cost. He paid the price for our sins, even though He did not sin, and freely gives us eternal life if we will simply accept the gift from Him and allow Him to be our Savior and Lord. Our hope is built on the blood and righteousness of Jesus. We have our very life and spiritual existence because Jesus died on the cross. By paying the penalty for our sins, the work of salvation was done; it was finished. Anyone and everyone who hungers for real life can believe in Jesus Christ, and thus obtain eternal life: drink from the springs of the water of life. And it costs us nothing. Salvation is free!

Going to church does not make us Christians. Hanging around Christians does not make us Christians. Performing religious acts does not make us Christians. Only by accepting the free gift of eternal life from Jesus and inviting Him to come into our hearts and lives can we be saved and partake of the water of life without cost.

If you have done this, you have the necessary cornerstone in your life to partake of these precepts, and practice the Alpha Omega Paradigm. If you have not, I invite you now to become a Christian. Pray this prayer right now, and you will be born again and begin establishing your permanent connections in God.

"Dear Jesus, thank you for dying on the Cross for me. Please forgive my sins and come into my heart and life. I step down from the throne of my heart, and ask you to sit there. I will drink your water of eternal life. Help me make the connections I need, so that I can live the abundant life you want me to live. I accept that I am saved by faith and grace. I love you Lord. Amen."

Part Two

Indwelling

Precept #1:
Connect to God inside of you.

Chapter Four

WHAT IS GOD?

God is inside of you! From the first to the last, God's presence in you is guaranteed. After you are saved, Jesus Christ is inside of you, and the better you connect with Him – inside – the better your whole Christian walk will go.

Through the years I have taught so many things from the Bible – so many really great things! And I have researched the deeper, weightier, meatier doctrines of the Word. I truly love studying the Bible. But this simple truth – the indwelling of God – is the deepest truth I have found in the New Covenant. It is so precious, yet so misunderstood. People act as if God is everywhere except inside of them! But connecting with Jesus inside of each one of us is the key to our deepest relationship with God and to our sensing, understanding and walking in the spiritual dimension. That's why this is Precept #1 in the Alpha Omega Paradigm.

To grasp the significance of God being inside of every Christian, consider first the question: What is God? Now I can hear almost everyone saying to me, "God is not a what; He is a who!" Please humor me and consider my question. I know God is a person, not a thing, but just humor me as we look at our Alpha Omega base Scriptures. In these passages of Scripture Jesus Christ helps us focus on what He is to our lives.

Revelation 1:8 – "I am the Alpha and the Omega," says the Lord God, "who is and who was and who is to come, the Almighty."

Revelation 21:6 – Then He said to me, "It is done. I am the Alpha and the Omega, the beginning and the end. I will give to the one who thirsts from the spring of the water of life without cost."

Revelation 22:13 – I am the Alpha and the Omega, the first and the last, the beginning and the end.

The saying, "I am the Alpha and the Omega" is found only these three times in the Bible. This is Jesus Christ, the Almighty God speaking. He wants to remind us of the simple truth that everything has a beginning and an ending: a church service, a course in college, a football game, a career, a love affair, a marriage, a broken leg, a Thanksgiving dinner, a movie, a war, a city council meeting, a concert, a bath or shower, an apple pie; anything and everything in our lives has a beginning and an ending.

I joined the U.S. army when I was eighteen, and was trained to be a basic soldier and a combat medic. When I hiked through the jungles in Viet Nam and Cambodia in 1970, I carried an M-16 rifle, as well as my medic kit. During basic training I received training in using both the M-14 and the M-16 rifle. Both rifles can fire "semi-automatic" and "automatic." Semi-automatic fires one bullet every time you squeeze the trigger; automatic fires many rounds with one squeeze of the trigger, depending upon how long you keep the trigger squeezed. In order for the rifle to perform in this manner, it must throw the bullet shell out of the way. The metal shells were called "brass." Rifles are designed for a right-handed person to fire, and the brass is thrown out of the way, harmlessly over to the right of the right-handed person firing. Well, I'm left-handed. When I would fire the rifle left-handed, the brass would be thrown back to the right and hit me in the face and right shoulder. It was a circumstance that they called, "eating the brass." My instructor recommended strongly that I learn to fire right-handed in order to avoid eating the brass. I first received training on the older rifle, the M-14. I took the instructor's advice and did the best I could firing right-handed. Since I am not very good at doing anything right-handed, I barely qualified as a "marksman." Back when I was being trained that was the lowest rating I could get and still pass. A few weeks later I received training on the M-16. This time I went against the instructor's advice and did the best I could firing left-handed. I had to fight through all the brass hitting me in the face (believe me, it could sting!), but I qualified as a "sharpshooter." That was the highest rating I could get. When I arrived in-country in Viet Nam, they gave me the traditional medic weapon, a .45 revolver. I fired thirty rounds with it on the test range and couldn't hit anything, so I begged them to give me an M-16 rifle, and they did. We had a standard joke in Viet Nam: if the enemy was close enough to use a .45 revolver, then club him! In any action I acted as a regular soldier, firing my M-16 as needed, up until someone got wounded and the call went out for, "Medic!" Forty-five years later, it is hard for people in the church to imagine me firing an M-16 in combat, but I was pretty good at it; especially firing 2-3 round blasts with accuracy. So what's my point?

**God designed you to have Him as your
Alpha and Omega in everything.**

Everything that we do and experience in life has a beginning and an ending. How we start has a major impact on how we finish. When I went through training on the M-14, I started wrong by doing it right-handed. That's not how God designed me: I'm a leftie! I finished the training poorly as a marksman, barely passing by the skin of my teeth. When I went through training on the M-16, I started right by doing it left-handed. That's how God designed me: I'm a leftie! I finished the training excellently as a sharp shooter, well-equipped for battle in Viet Nam and Cambodia. So too is life as a Christian: whatever you do, if you start right with Jesus Christ you are going to finish excellently. God designed you to have Him as your Alpha and Omega in everything. In whatever situation or circumstance, ask yourself: do you want to come out as a marksman or a sharp shooter? The precepts of the Alpha Omega Paradigm will equip you from the beginning to finish excellently. So ask yourself: What is God? He is your Alpha and Omega, your best beginning and ending in everything.

So that uncomfortable question I asked: What is God? God is inside of you and the better you connect with Him within you, the better your whole Christian walk will go. He is Alpha and Omega inside of you. I said this was the simple and deepest truth of the New Testament that I have found. But we do need to accept this truth. God in His fullness is within every Christian.

Colossians 2:9 – For in Him all the fullness of Deity dwells in bodily form,…

God in His fullness is within every Christian. This verse makes it clear that Jesus Christ has the fullness of Deity in Him. Our God is eternally existent in three persons: God the Father, God the Son and God the Holy Spirit. We like to express it like this: God is one in three – three in one. He is one God in three persons – three persons in one God. Let's break this verse down a little more.

In **Him** – refers to Jesus Christ.

All the **fullness of Deity** – refers to the Godhead, the Trinity: the Father and the Son and the Holy Spirit.

Dwells – refers to living in; having one's abode in. The verb is a present tense, so when Paul wrote the Epistle to the church in Colossae (A.D. 60-61), the fullness of the Godhead was dwelling in Jesus Christ. We understand from other Scripture that the fullness of God was within Jesus as He walked this earth. But this Scripture is not referring to the past, when Jesus Christ walked the earth in His physical body (4 B.C. – A.D. 29). It is referring to a later time in the church age. We are still in the church age, and the fullness of the Godhead dwells in Jesus Christ right now.

In **bodily form** – Jesus Christ made the same transition as every human does at death. He went from His physical body/container to His spiritual body/container. He now has a spiritual dimension container, and the fullness of the Godhead is now dwelling in Him. I'll tell you now: I don't understand this. I accept it, but I don't understand it.

John 4:24 – God is spirit, and those who worship Him must worship in spirit and truth.

There are many things that I don't understand. If God is spirit, how can He be inside Jesus Christ in bodily form? And why is He inside Jesus Christ in bodily form? I don't know, and I am aware that there are many things about God that I don't know or understand. When Christ comes back at the Second Coming, I will probably learn a lot of things and increase tremendously in knowledge. What I do know now is that Jesus Christ is in every Christian believer, and the fullness of the Godhead is in Him. Therefore the fullness of the Godhead is inside of every Christian believer, including me.

I'm not going to explain the Trinity because I am confident you accept the doctrine, just as most Christians have for 2,000 years. And I accept it just as you do, even though I can't fully comprehend it. But I don't accept our practice of dividing the Godhead. We seem to practice that God the Father is in heaven, and God the Son ascended into heaven back in the first century, about ten days before the Holy Spirit came on the Day of Pentecost. And now the Holy Spirit dwells inside of us. So when we send prayers and praise to the Father, we send them "up" into heaven, where Christ is, seated at the right hand of the Father, always making intercession for us. When we relate to Jesus, once again, we look "up" into the heavens, and petition Him to intercede for our sins. Then when we want to relate to God inside of us, we talk to the Spirit of God. We seem to relate to God in thirds. Yet the Holy Spirit "super-intercedes" for us, according to Romans 8:26. So the fullness of the Godhead dwells in Jesus, the Son, in bodily form. That means that all of God: the Father, the Son and the Holy Spirit is inside of Jesus, and He is inside of us. The fullness of the Godhead is inside each of us; not just one-third of God. You are probably saying, "What's the big deal?" Well, God is the Alpha and the Omega. He is God the Father, God the Son and God the Holy Spirit. I want us to wrap our minds around what God is, so that we can better understand and appreciate the indwelling of God – that simple truth that I also said was the deepest I have found in the New Covenant.

Chapter Five

WHERE IS GOD?

We move to the next question: Where is God?

Exodus 40:34-38 – Then the cloud covered the tent of meeting, and the glory of the LORD filled the tabernacle. Moses was not able to enter the tent of meeting because the cloud had settled on it, and the glory of the LORD filled the tabernacle. Throughout all their journeys whenever the cloud was taken up from over the tabernacle, the sons of Israel would set out; but if the cloud was not taken up then they did not set out until the day when it was taken up. For throughout all their journeys, the cloud of the LORD was on the tabernacle by day, and there was fire on it by night, in the sight of all the house of Israel.

14,400 days. This was a miracle, every day.

What an extraordinary circumstance! During the time that the Israelites wandered in the wilderness for forty years, God's presence was manifested to them in the form of a cloud and fire. A cloud covered the tent of meeting and the glory of the LORD filled the tabernacle. So long as the cloud stay settled on the tabernacle the nation would stay in place. If the cloud lifted up, the Israelites would break camp and move wherever God would direct them. That cloud was always there over the tabernacle by day, and at night it turned into fire. Even though there were 2 ½ — 3 million people in the camp, day or night they could always look toward the tabernacle in the middle of the encampment and see the cloud or the fire. It was a huge encampment, and it was a large cloud or fire. God was present with them in the tabernacle for over forty years; over 14,400 days. This was a miracle, every day, for the whole time. Where was God? For them, at that time, His presence was in the tabernacle.

II Chronicles 7:1-3 — Now when Solomon had finished praying, fire came down from heaven and consumed the burnt offering and the sacrifices, and the glory of the LORD filled the house. The priests could not enter into the house of the LORD because the glory of the LORD filled the LORD's house. All the sons of Israel, seeing the fire come down and the glory of the LORD upon the house, bowed down on the pavement with their faces to the ground, and they worshipped and gave praise to the LORD, saying, "Truly He is good, truly His lovingkindness is everlasting."

When the Israelites were established in the Holy Land, their third King, Solomon, son of David, built the beautiful, glorious temple of the LORD. It became famous throughout the known world. People came from near and far to see it, even the Queen of Sheba. At the dedication service the LORD sent fire from heaven and the glory of the LORD filled the temple. The presence of the LORD was in the temple. For the Israelites every time they had a special feast they had to come to the temple in Jerusalem to be near the presence of the LORD. When King Solomon died, he was succeeded by his son Rehoboam (I Kings chapters 12-14). Because Rehoboam foolishly continued taxing all the Israelites heavily, there was a revolt, and ten of the tribes broke away under a new king: Jereboam. The ten tribes formed the northern kingdom, Israel, under King Jereboam, while two tribes stayed under King Rehoboam in the southern kingdom, Judah. The city of Jerusalem and the temple of the LORD were part of the southern kingdom. It was still important that all of the Israelites come to Jerusalem because the presence of the LORD was there. Prior to the revolt, a prophet of God had told Jereboam that if he would serve the LORD and follow His statutes and ordinances, he would be rewarded with a great established and prosperous nation. Now even though the kingdoms were split into north and south, the people still had to come to the temple in Jerusalem to worship the LORD. King Jereboam knew that coming to the place of the presence of the LORD was important and necessary for the Israelites, but he feared that if the people went to Jerusalem, they would reconsider and go back to Rehoboam. Even though he had the promise of God that his kingdom would be established and prosper, he went against God's statutes and ordinances. He made two golden calves, set them up at two cities in his northern kingdom and declared a feast to take place at the same time that there was supposed to be a feast in Jerusalem, centered around the temple, where God's presence dwelled. That doomed the northern kingdom to have wicked kings and idolatry throughout the years, and led God's people away from the presence of the LORD. So where was God during all those years that Solomon's temple existed? For all of the Israelites it was in the temple in Jerusalem. The contention as to where God was to be worshipped still existed hundreds of years later, as we read about the interaction between Jesus and the woman at the well in Samaria (John chapter four).

John 4:21 – Jesus said to her, "Woman, believe Me, an hour is coming when neither in this mountain nor in Jerusalem will you worship the Father.

John 4:23 – But an hour is coming, and now is, when the true worshipers will worship the Father in spirit and truth; for such people the Father seeks to be His worshipers.

I Corinthians 3:16 – Do you not know that you are a temple of God and that the Spirit of God dwells in you?

So in the Old Testament we see the presence of the LORD first in the Tabernacle, then secondly in Solomon's Temple. But in the New Covenant we are the temple and He dwells inside of us, corporately and individually.

*Matthew 18:19, 20 – Again I say to you, that if two of you agree on earth about anything that they may ask, it shall be done for them by My Father who is in heaven. For where two or three have gathered together in My name, **I am there in their midst.***

Jesus Christ dwells in us corporately. Where two or three (or more) are gathered together in the name of the Lord Jesus Christ He is there in the midst of them. That's God's presence in His temple (the group of Christians!). But some have said that God is not present when we are alone, but only when we are with other Christians. That is not what Jesus was saying!

I Corinthians 6:18-20 – Flee immorality. Every other sin that a man commits is outside the body, but the immoral man sins against his own body. Or do you not know that your body is a temple of the Holy Spirit who is in you, whom you have from God, and that you are not your own? For you have been bought with a price: therefore glorify God in your body.

This makes clear that the Holy Spirit dwells in every Christian individually. The context is exhorting individual Christians not to commit sexual sin/fornication/adultery. Individuals! Get it? God is inside every individual Christian. Scripture overwhelmingly teaches that God is within each individual Christian.

*Matthew 28:20 – teaching them to observe all that I commanded you; and lo, I am **with you always,** even to the end of the age.*

*John 14:16, 17 – I will ask the Father, and He will give you another Helper, that He may be with you forever; that is the Spirit of truth, whom the world cannot receive, because it does not see Him or know Him; but you know Him because He abides with you **and will be in you.***

*I John 4:4 – You are from God, little children, and have **overcome** them; because **greater is He who is in you** than he who is in the world.*

*John 15:4 – **Abide in Me, and I in you.** As the branch cannot bear fruit of itself unless it abides in the vine, so neither can you unless you abide in Me. I am the vine, you are the branches; he who **abides in Me and I in him,** he **bears much fruit,** for apart from Me you can do nothing*

*John 17:21, 23 – that they may all be one; even as you, **Father, are in Me and I in You, that they also may be in Us,** so that the world may believe that You sent Me…**I in them and You in Me,** that they may be perfected in **unity,** so that the world may know that You sent Me, and loved them, even as You have loved Me.*

*Romans 8:10, 11 – If Christ is **in you,** though the body is dead because of sin, yet the spirit is alive because of righteousness. But if the Spirit of Him who raised Jesus from the dead **dwells in you,** He who raised Christ Jesus from the dead will also give life to your mortal bodies through His Spirit who **dwells in you.***

Jesus promised that He would always be with us. He said another Comforter, the Spirit of truth, was with the disciples and would be in them. He said that God who is in us is greater than the devil in the world. That's why we overcome the evil one. He commanded us to abide in Him, just as He abides in us. That connection results in us producing the fruit that He wants and that we want. He prayed for us that we would have unity; like the unity He has with the Father. He is in the Father, the Father is in Him, and He is in us. That makes all of God in us! He emphasized strongly that Christ is in each Christian and in the same Scripture verse He said that the Spirit dwells in each Christian.

God indwelling us has a timeline progression. It starts with the moment of salvation and keeps on going. It is all about abiding, just as the branches and the vine are strongly connected. The strong abiding connection Jesus talks about in John chapter fifteen is not some simple slip joint. I work regularly with a lap top computer, and I often pull my computer loose from its power connection, because I pull it around too hard, and the connection is a pretty simple pop in – pop out connection. Not too long ago I managed a recycling project that had these big, fully automated machines for recycling bottles and cans. Inside there was a computer that connected to everything: from customer interfaces to screen displays to electric eyes to automated conveyors. Interestingly enough all those cables and connections did not come loose. In fact it was hard to get them disconnected because on either side of the pop in – pop out cable connections were two screws that went deeply into the body of the piece of machinery. It was a solid connection, staying tight and not coming loose. That's the kind of abiding connection that the vine and the branches are to have (from John chapter fifteen). That's the kind of connection that we have with God: He is in us and we are in Him! It is cemented in the unity that we have with God; it is a solid connection for the purpose of letting the world know that the Lord Jesus Christ is for them, loves them and wants to connect with them. When we really understand that God is in us we have fruit and healing from God, and by presenting the gospel to everyone in the world every person has the same chance to have healing and fruit in Jesus.

Chapter Six

JUST SAY HELLO!

I have developed a quick and simple process to connect with God inside of me. At any time of the day I will pause and say, "Hello, Jesus." At that moment I am in contact with Him. Sometimes I feel it, sometimes I don't. But I know that I am aware of Him and we are connected. And then we talk. That's the awesome reality.

That term "hello" has as interesting history. It comes out of the 1800's. References throughout the century give us insight.

- 1803   an exclamation to call attention, an expression of surprise, or a greeting.

- 1840   to shout or an exclamation originally shouted in a hunt when the quarry was spotted

- 1877   Thomas Edison made it popular as a telephone greeting

- 1883   (referring to approximately 1400) a shout to attract attention

- 1889   central telephone exchange operators were known as 'hello-girls' due to the association between the greeting and the telephone.

The word was in popular use as a greeting and a beginning of conversation at the same time that the telephone started coming into use. As the phone was used more and more, it was standard that the conversation began with the word, "Hello." In the places where there were lady attendants/operators responding to incoming requests and connecting appropriate lines, those operators were called, "Hello-girls." For me it has become a simple and easy way to connect to the real God inside of me, and converse.

Connect with Him inside of you. Don't make it complicated; just say "Hello, Jesus." At that point in time you are connected! It's just that easy to get started. Embrace the reality that the Lord Jesus Christ is in you and rejoice in what His inner presence provides:

You and Jesus are the most powerful team in the spiritual dimension.

Protection – The moment you say "Hello" to Jesus within you, you are operating in the spiritual dimension. Instead of being afraid of the devil and his demons, you can calmly live and communicate in the heavenlies. After all, Jesus is in you and you and Jesus are the most powerful team in the spiritual dimension. You are protected from the devil!

Peace – You don't need to have any fear or confusion. God always wants us to move forward in faith, while Satan constantly tries to stir our fear. God is never the author of confusion, while Satan seems to throw anything and everything he can in front of us to distract and to bring confusion. God always has the advantage because He is inside of us. There is nothing as calm, peaceful and full of faith as being in touch with God within you. He's there all the time with His peace that passes our understanding. But even if we can't understand His peace, we can partake of it!

Power – When you doubt you can do something (I can't do it) or you're afraid to do something (I might fail), just remind yourself to connect with God who is within you. Avoid the biggest lie Satan tries to bring. He lies by getting us to think: "Even if God has the power, He is not going to use it for us; He is going to withhold the power." Jesus came solidly against this lie of the devil when He said:

Luke 11:13 – If you then, being evil, know how to give good gifts to your children, how much more will your heavenly Father give the Holy Spirit to those who ask Him?

Matthew 6:11 – If you then, being evil, know how to give good gifts to your children, how much more shall your Father who is in heaven give what is good to those who ask Him!

He is the LORD God Almighty. He is Jehovah and El Shaddai. Nobody comes close to His power. Because He is within you, His power is available to you.

Paraphernalia – equipment, resources, gifts, memory recall; whatever you need to get the job done, whatever the mission is, God who is inside of you has all the supplies you need. You need His gifting to accomplish the mission; you need "stuff" to get the various ministry tasks done; you need to remember what He has said to you, what He has promised for you; all the equipment, weapons and ammunition is available for you from your God who is within you.

Possessions – Now come on; you know that we obsess over having enough money, enough food, enough clothing, enough "stuff." I understand that we need to learn to abase and abound, and to be good stewards. But we can quit worrying about any of it. God is within us, and it all belongs to Him. As the old song said, "He owns the cattle on a thousand hills, the wealth of every mine." Have you noticed that when you tithe, you still have 90%, to be a good steward of? And the Scriptures declare that we are joint heirs with Jesus. Whatever He owns, we are heirs! Pretty rich, huh?

Did you see that all my points started with a "P"? I guess I learned something in my Homiletics classes! Thanks go to my professor, Dr. Pecota! O.K., let's wrap this up.

- God in His fullness is inside of each of us! Our Alpha and Omega in every circumstance and situation is inside of each of us.

- Be aware that God is within each of us! It's like we have a switch we can turn on that makes us aware of God within, and we connect with Him, and we communicate with Him. How often do we turn the switch off? Why do we leave the switch off most of the time? God is within each of us...let's keep the switch of awareness on!

- Let's connect with Him! The Alpha Omega Paradigm is all about connections. The Christian life must have all the strong connections God has prepared for us.

- Let's use our advantage! Look at it this way. If this Christian life can be compared to a wrestling match, who is our ultimate tag team partner? It is the Lord Jesus Christ within every one of us.

So in this first connection we consider our Holy Spirit legend. What is the will of the Holy Spirit? He is establishing your heart as His home, where He resides. He loves you, so He enjoys being in you. And He loves receiving your love. He wants you to enjoy His presence within you, to give Him a hug once in awhile and express your love to Him. To each one of us He is saying: "I'm here in your heart all the time. Enjoy My presence and love Me as I love you." What a legend we have!

I was raised in a Pentecostal Church, and have ministered in charismatic and restoration churches over many years. But I have heard of something called "catechism" that some of the older, more traditional churches practice in teaching and training their people. The catechism usually takes the form of a question and correct answer that people memorize. I want to use that simple idea to conclude each precept, as we emphasize it. It will be like this. Imagine that the Lord, or your spiritual leader, or me, as the author of this book is asking you the question, out loud. Give the answer, out loud, and do it several times. I have found that this helps the people that I teach to remember and embrace the precepts of the Lord. So here it is:

Catechism

Question: Where is God?

Answer: Inside of me, and also everywhere.

Part Three

The Church, At Church, In Church

Precept #2:
Connect to your Church

Chapter Seven

THE CHURCH IS...A BUNCH OF BONES

In the second half of the 20th century there were exciting happenings and movements among Christians: the Charismatic Movement, the Jesus People Movement, Shepherding, Restoration, Five-Fold Ministry, etc., that brought a fresh breath of the Holy Spirit to the church. But as with all things that humans are involved in, while many Christians handled these things in a decent, orderly and edifying way, there were some excesses and errors. Some leaders tried to exercise excessive authority; some Christians acted unseemly and overly emotional, resulting in Christians being hurt; some were even betrayed by church leaders. Some people felt that the church and church leaders were trying to boss them around and control them. An unfortunate way of relating to God developed and continued into our present times: let's call it the "Just me and Jesus Syndrome." People lost their trust in churches, church leaders and pastors, so they believed that all they needed was to commune directly with Jesus. Now if we go back to the first century church, as described in the Book of Acts and in the Epistles, we find that they were humans, and that there were excesses and errors. Even leaders had arguments and disagreements. But we do not see some of them rejecting the church, as has happened in our time. There is no

Scriptural support for individual Christians living their lives without the church. To the contrary, God makes it clear that everyone of us is part of His church and therefore we need to connect properly to the church. This connection is critical for every Christian, young or old in the Christian walk. Let's consider the Biblical pattern.

So, what is the church?

The Church is...A Bunch of Bones

Ezekiel 37:1-10 – The hand of the Lord was upon me, and He brought me out by the Spirit of the LORD and set me down in the middle of the valley; and it was full of bones. He caused me to pass among them round about, and behold, there were very many on the surface of the valley; and lo, they were very dry. He said to me, "Son of man, can these bones live?" And I answered, "O Lord GOD, You know." Again He said to me, "Prophesy over these bones and say to them, 'O dry bones, hear the word of the LORD.' Thus says the Lord GOD to these bones, 'Behold, I will cause breath to enter you that you may come to life. I will put sinews on you, make flesh grow back on you, cover you with skin and put breath in you that you may come alive; and you will know that I am the LORD.'" So I prophesied as I was commanded; and as I prophesied, there was a noise, and behold, a rattling; and the bones came together, bone to its bone. And I looked, and behold, sinews were on them, and flesh grew and skin covered them; but there was no breath in them. Then He said to me, prophesy, son of man, and say to the breath, – Thus says the Lord GOD, "Come from the four winds, O breath, and breathe on these slain, that they come to life.'" So I prophesied as He commanded me, and the breath came into them, and they came to life and stood on their feet, an exceedingly great army.

This was an Old Testament prophecy given through Ezekiel about the restoration of the house of Israel. In God's

Scripture pattern of Old Testament shadow being New Testament substance, this is giving us a picture of the New Testament church of Jesus Christ. In the following verse fourteen, God says, "I will put my Spirit within you, and you will come to life..." It is in the New Covenant, the New Testament, when individuals become Christians, that God's Spirit is within each of us, so this Old Testament prophecy is a picture of the New Testament church.

Back in May of 2012, my wife and I were privileged to take a two-week driving vacation in Ireland and Scotland. Jan became an excellent navigator, while I concentrated on the new concept of driving on the left side of the road, with the steering wheel in the front right seat. I became proficient, although I kept scarring the tires and wheels on curbs. Good thing I got the complete insurance coverage! During the vacation time I asked the Lord to give me a special word of prophecy for my home church, VLife Church, back in McKinney, Texas. God answered my prayers and gave me a specific word based upon this Ezekiel vision of the valley of dry bones.

In this vision, God showed Ezekiel a valley that was full of scattered, dry bones. God took him through the process by which the bones became a living, great army for the Lord. As Ezekiel prophesied over the bones, they came together, connecting into proper skeletons. God put sinews, flesh and skin onto the bones, and then He breathed on them. God's Spirit came into them and they stood on their feet, a very great army. Sounds awesome, doesn't it?

God showed me something in this prophecy that I had not seen before. I had always viewed everything about the bones becoming an army as the result of the supernatural touch of God's Spirit. But in reality, God did some of it, and the bones did some of it. Applying that to the church, God does some and we do some, in order for us to become the mighty army of God.

God puts the sinews, flesh and skin on the body, and He breathes life into it by His Spirit. Without question God's part is the most important: flesh and blood and muscles given the breath of life. But take a look at what we (the bones) do.

When I stopped the rattling, you could hear a pin drop.

The bones came together. There was a noise, a rattling, and the bones came together, bone to its bone. Can you imagine what that must have sounded like? The last time I taught on this, I put several Lego's into a Tupperware container and held it very close to the microphone. Then I shook it; first gently, then stronger, then as hard as I could. It filled the whole auditorium with a loud, noisy rattling. The congregation was startled, and when I stopped the rattling, you could hear a pin drop. It was a memorable auditory illustration to cement the concept of bones coming into place. When the bones came together (bone to its bone) the rattling noise filled the whole valley. So too, when Christians in their churches come together, joined with other Christians in the right place to do the will of the Lord and accomplish their great work of the ministry, it creates a great sound in the world. It's the sound of church people connecting together in unity to show everyone the gospel of Jesus Christ. God has designed His church in a way that requires individuals connecting. Jesus expressed this very well when He spoke the "two or three" principle in Matthew.

*Matthew 18:19, 20 — Again I say to you, that if two of you agree on earth about anything that they may ask, it shall be done for them by My Father who is in heaven. For where **two or three** have gathered together in My name, I am there in their midst.*

Every Christian needs to look for the special one or two that God is joining them to within their church. In my local church I have the opportunity from time to time to teach and preach. I am a disabled veteran (damaged legs and back). I get around with a walker, but in the old church building there are steps up to the platform, and I cannot get up there by myself. Every time the pastor has me speak, as he is introducing me, without exception, two or three of the brothers step forward and help me up the steps and into the chair from which I speak. I kid you not, every time. This is just one excellent example of "two or three." Recently I had a more unusual, but very encouraging example of "two or three." A young man name Kyle came up to me and told me he had spoken with our Pastor, who directed him to come and talk with me. Kyle said that recently he had a repetitive dream (five or six times) and I was in it. He didn't understand why he was having the dream and that's why he had talked with Pastor Mike. In the dream Kyle had seen me walking, unassisted, up the outside front steps of the church; fourteen cement steps. Without a miracle healing there is no way that I could do that. I believe in divine healing; I have had many people lay hands on me and pray for me to be healed, and I pray for God to heal me. I want to be able to run again; nothing fancy, just jogging two or three miles in the evening. I haven't been healed yet, but God is able and I am willing. The point is that Kyle sharing that dream with me had a wonderful, calming effect. It greatly encouraged me because I do believe that one day it will happen. That unusual interaction between Kyle and I over his dreams is another excellent example of the "two or three" principle. The bones have to come together, bone to its bone.

It's not enough for an individual Christian to attend Sunday morning mass meetings, but not connect. God wants every Christian individual to connect to his "bone" in the church.

The bones stood up. They stood on their feet as an exceedingly great army. The completion of the vision was fantastic. God had performed the miracle and everybody came alive. Then all these individuals stood up. When individual Christians have flesh and blood and muscles from God, and the breath of life from His Spirit, they must stand up. Away with the couches and recliners: on your feet, people!

They didn't just stand up. Can you see thousands of bodies just standing up, anywhere and everywhere in the valley? You have undoubtedly heard of huge crowds in some auditorium suddenly trying to get out because of a fire, or a bomb threat. They get tangled, the door gets plugged, and people get trampled. It's not enough for thousands of people to just stand up. There's got to be some type of order. The bone bodies stood up as an exceedingly great army. When an army stands up, they have a formation; there is rank and file. Each soldier stands in his squad. Each squad stands in its platoon. Each platoon stands in its company. Each company stands in its brigade. When there is order like that, the army can follow orders efficiently and move quickly. Every individual Christian needs to stand with his ministry team, in their ministry group, in the local church God has placed them in. That results in efficiency, order and quick movement in accomplishing the work of the ministry.

The church is…a bunch of bones. Let's each one of us connect to one another like God intends, and move with our team and group and local church to be what God wants us to be and do what He wants us to do.

Chapter Eight

THE CHURCH IS...HIS BODY

I Corinthians 12:12-18 – For even as the body is one and yet has many members, and all the members of the body, though they are many, are one body, so also is Christ. For by one Spirit we were all baptized into one body, whether Jews or Greeks, whether slaves or free, and we were all made to drink of one Spirit. For the body is not one member, but many. If the foot says, "Because I am not a hand, I am not a part of the body," it is not for this reason any the less a part of the body. – And if the ear says, "Because I am not an eye, I am not a part of the body," it is not for this reason any the less a part of the body. If the whole body were an eye, where would the hearing be? If the whole were hearing, where would the sense of smell be? But now God has placed the members, each one of them, in the body, just as He desired.

In teaching the Corinthian church about spiritual gifts, how varied they could be and how they were to use them in operating together, Paul uses the human body as an illustration of how a local church works and inter-relates. The foot can't say it's not a hand, so it's not a part of the body; the ear can't say it's not an eye, so it's not a part of the body. Regardless of what the foot and ear say, they are still part of the body. The whole body can't be an eye; if it were there would be no hearing (or for that matter any of the other functions of a body). If the whole body was one big hearing ear, there would be no sense of smell. A body can't work that way. Each part needs to do what it was designed for. So it is with the church. It is the body of Christ, and needs to function the proper way.

This Scripture gives us four important points of body life and function.

1. Be the member God has made you. If you embrace what God has made you in the body, you will fulfill what God has in mind, namely, your unique work of the ministry.

God does not use Lone Rangers.

---

2. God does not use Lone Rangers. Christians who think that they can fulfill the will of God all by themselves, end up thwarting God's best plan for their lives, for the church's vitality and for the world's salvation. That sounds strong, but it is true. Lone Rangers think of themselves more highly than they ought to think, exhibiting pride and arrogance. When they try to join themselves to a church, they often come with that arrogance still in place. They come in acting and speaking something like this: "I want to do this ministry in this church, I know it's what I should do, and if you don't let me do this, then you're wrong and I'm leaving!" This Scripture teaches clearly that attitude and arrogance like this will not work in the body of Christ (the church). There's no place for Lone Rangers in the church.

3. We can't all do the same thing. Presently in your church and mine, there are certain gifts that are more in the limelight; one might even say these gifts are more fun because everyone sees them and likes them. As a result, people want to use those gifts. But we can't all do the same thing. We can't all be prophets and teachers; we can't all be worship musicians, etc. For me specifically, over the years God has gifted me in prophecy and teaching. Right now He has placed me in a church where the pastor is strong as a Prophet and Teacher. I could be saying, "Listen to me. Let me have the opportunities to minister in teaching and prophecy too." But how many voices can you have in the church, prophesying and teaching? If we all do that, then the other ministries and gifts, which are equally needed, get neglected, and the church limps along, instead of running with the Spirit of God. I have found that God is using my wife and I a lot just to pray for people and speak a word of knowledge or a word of wisdom, as the Spirit directs. There are also times when the pastor requests that I teach on a particular thing, and I do whatever he directs me to do. The variety of gifts and ministries in the church are all needed and blend together to further His kingdom and His righteousness.

4. God has placed the members, each one of them, just as He desired. Think about the church you are in. Why did you choose your church? Why is it your church home? When someone is looking for their church home, the pastor of every church that they check out has an inclination to believe that they should choose his church to attend. I have pastored a few churches and I know whereof I speak. When Christians have asked me for help in choosing a church, I have often

suggested they make a list of ten things their home church must have. Then I have told them to pick which three are the most important, and use those to help them in the decision. But here's the bottom line. No matter what you think happened when you chose your church home, if it is where God wants you to be, then He is the one who has placed you there. If you can wrap your mind and will around that, then you will fit in and minister according to His will.

Let's look at a couple more Scriptures:

Ephesians 4:16 – from whom the whole body, being fitted and held together by what every joint supplies, according to the proper working of each individual part, causes the growth of the body, for the building up of itself in love.

Fitting and working leads to growing and building. The church (the body of Christ) works that way. I recall a good illustration from my past. I was watching a special program on PBS that gave the story of how some particular skyscraper building was erected. They showed a time lapse of the building going up: from the deep digging of foundations, through the erection of all those metal beams, then the other materials being added in. It all went incredibly fast and the end result was this fantastic skyscraper building. It showed all kinds of fitting and working, and the edifice was growing and building until completion. That's how it is supposed to be for the church, the body of Christ.

Ephesians 1:22 – And He put all things in subjection under His feet, and gave Him as head over all things to the church, which is His body, the fullness of Him who fills all in all.

This is a profound and compelling concept. The church (the body) is the fullness of Him. Jesus Christ is the master operator, from creation, through construction, to completion, He fills all in all. He created everything. He was there in the beginning (Remember, He is your Alpha and Omega). He directs it all; all the way through. He has chosen to express His fullness through the church. Because of Him, and because He is doing the filling, the church is a super fantastic, profound and compelling thing. He will accomplish everything that He has designed to come to pass, and He has chosen to do it in and through the church.

The church is...His body. Find where God has placed you in the body: find your local church. Then discover what part of the body God has made you to be, and be that part, do that work of the ministry, so that God's kingdom and God's righteousness are done. That's how you connect to the church.

Chapter Nine

THE CHURCH IS...A BUILDING

Ephesians 2:19-22 – So then you are no longer strangers and aliens, but you are fellow citizens with the saints, and are of God's household, having been built on the foundation of the apostles and prophets, Christ Jesus Himself being the cornerstone, in whom the whole building, being fitted together, is growing into a holy temple in the Lord, in whom you also are being built together into a dwelling of God in the Spirit.

Sounds very familiar doesn't it? Building and fitting together, growing and being built together; the language Scripture uses in describing how the body of Christ works. Here the language is clearly painting a picture of a significant building. Let's look at the significant building points:

1. For the building to develop into a great temple, it must have the right foundation and cornerstone. A social cornerstone will never work. Social needs vary and what people think is important can change. Just look at the issue of gay marriage over the last ten years. What a staggering change in the attitude and opinions of people. Remember the Defense of Marriage Act passed by Congress? How quickly social positions change. Which way is the public opinion wind blowing? Which people can spend how much money

to bring about "political correctness?" Men and their social opinions can and do change. We must have a cornerstone that is stationary and unchanging. Our Lord Jesus Christ is the same, yesterday, today and forever. That's a cornerstone! But what about the foundation? Are there Apostles and Prophets in the church today to make the right foundation? There were many apostles in the New Testament church: certainly more than the original twelve. And the apostles and prophets of the New Testament church were part and parcel of the ministry and body function in the church. That is needed, and thankfully present, in the church today. An apostle leads, directs and covers the church, and often performs that function for multiple churches. The right kind of direction and correction is needed in the church today, just as it was needed in the church of the first century. Instead of denying the work of apostles and prophets today, let's stop fighting that truth; identify who they are, consider the results of their ministry, and benefit from their direction and covering.

2. If it's a building, we are built **together.** When Jesus walked this earth, He is the one who expressed the "two or three" principle. The strength that comes out of that concept is being **together**, coming into **agreement**, and thus experiencing and expressing **unity**. Remember what we said about the valley of dry bones. What is the sound in our camp, in our local church? Is it the sound of partying, like Moses and Joshua heard when they came back down the mountain to find the Israelites singing, dancing and worshipping a golden calf? Is it the sound of murmuring, like Moses heard from his very own family? Or is it the huge sound of rattling. Rattle, rattle! Bones

coming together, aligned in their proper places to function and minister. To see, understand and release the power of God in our churches, we must first come together, and then come into agreement. We are a building and we are built together!

3. God dwells in the building, His church. This ties right into the first precept: the indwelling of God. He is inside each individual Christian. When we say, "Hello, Jesus," we are embracing and conversing with Jesus Christ inside each of us. When several of us get together, Jesus inside each individual is present in the whole group, the building, His church, in a special and stronger way. God dwells in your local church: the people.

In all these illustrations, the bones, the body, the building, we see the precept: Connect to your local church; not as a Sunday morning spectator, but as a connected, fully functioning body member, pressing into and accomplishing the special work of the ministry that He designed you to perform.

I'm still with Christ, but I am done with the church.

From the beginning of the 21st century, we have seen and heard more and more Christians saying something like this: I'm still with Christ, but I am done with the church." The case is often that someone has been hurt by an experience in the church. Perhaps a leader has fallen into sin; maybe someone in the church wronged them in business, or the church gossip line has eaten them alive. They are saying that they can get along just fine with Jesus, but they don't want to relate to church people anymore. The sad reality is that the church is made up of humans, and humans do wrong things, whether it is in the church, the Rotary Club, the social club, the work place or wherever. You don't hear people say: I'm still with me, but I am done with my work place." They don't quit their job, or their family, or their social organization because someone has wronged them. But they will quit the church. God knew that humans would be in His church, and would make mistakes. But Jesus Christ called it "His church." That means we don't have the option of dropping out. If you're done with the church, you're not going to get along with Christ, because He will be saying, again and again: "Time to get back in. Forgive, connect and grow." It is necessary and crucial that you connect to your local church.

The Church, at Church, In Church. I have used this phrase over the last year to remind myself of what the church is and how I am a part. The Church – reminds me that because Jesus Christ died for me on the Cross, and I have accepted Him by faith as my Savior and Lord, I am part of the church. At Church – reminds me that every time I gather in a particular building with other Christians, say on a Sunday morning, I am at church in the building. I have come together with my fellow Christians in that particular gathering place. In Church – reminds me that I have a responsibility to be aware of and reach out to all the Christians around me, when I am at Church. I don't just go to a service to block out everyone around me and focus on Jesus. With my soul and spirit I need to reach out to the Christians with me; that's being in church. It is at those moments that we can come into agreement. We have come together; we can come into agreement; we can have unity. The Church, at Church, in Church.

To our Holy Spirit legend again: What is the will of the Holy Spirit? He is the breath of life in each one of us individually, but also the breath of life in us corporately. That's how the bones with flesh and skin come to life. There is a special way that connected Christians have the life and breath of the Holy Spirit to enliven the group. That is what the Holy Spirit is doing. And He wants every one of us to connect with each other in the local churches that He has called into being, and designed to be successfully functioning groups. To each one of us He is saying, "You are an essential part of your local church. Find your local church, find your place in that church, connect solidly with your fellow Christians in that church, and minister for Jesus!"

So what is our catechism?

Catechism

Question:
What is the Church?

Answer:
We are; connected in the right local church where God has placed us.

Part Four

Your Elder, Your Shepherd, Your Pastor

Precept #3: Connect To Your Pastor

Chapter Ten

YOUR PASTOR: YOUR COVERING

Let's refresh our thoughts a bit. In the Alpha Omega Paradigm we look at things in a complete and continuing way. It's all about the right connections. A couple of points:

- In anything and everything, we need to make Jesus Christ the first thing, and continue to keep Him involved and paramount, even to the end. He promises to be there from the beginning to the end, if you let Him.

- There are certain **connections** that we need to practice in our Christian walk, from our spiritual birth to our spiritual maturity. We're never too old as Christians to practice these **connections.**

- We need to connect to Jesus Christ inside of us. Let me ask this question: Where is His throne room? We have a tendency to look up and away, to somewhere in the heavens, for the location of His throne. Somewhere there in heaven the Father is seated on His throne, and Jesus is seated at the right hand of the Father. But Scripture also teaches that we are seated with Him in the heavenlies, at the right hand of the Father. And when we accept Jesus as our Savior, we ask Him to come into our heart and sit on the throne of our heart to be our Lord. There is a specific way in which the throne room of Jesus is inside of us, where He is seated on the throne of our hearts as Savior and Lord.

- We need to connect to the church. We are the church and are to be connected together with other Christians in the local church, where God has placed us. By being connected to our fellow Christians, we serve well and fulfill the work of the ministry that God has planned for us.

Every one of us, new and old, needs to be connected to our pastor. He is our covering. The covering concept is understood and practiced throughout our society. Covering refers to something that protects, shelters, defends or guards. When we get insurance for our cars or houses, we say we are "covered." Parents cover their children; husbands cover their wives; a pastor covers his congregation. When my wife and I were discussing this concept, she brought up an illustration that she always thinks about in this context. If you have ever been on a farm with chickens, you can see how a hen covers and protects her baby chicks. She will be walking around the yard and her little chicks will follow her. There's always a lot of clucking and cheeping being heard. If the hen senses some danger she will cluck in a particular way, and all the little chicks will run and tuck themselves under mommy. She spreads her wings slightly and lowers herself to the ground and all the chicks are hidden. Now and then you will see a little head pop out to peek around, and then disappear back under mommy's wing. The hen covers her baby chicks, thus guarding, protecting and sheltering them. Great covering, huh? As I studied the practice of covering in the Bible, examining the Greek and Hebrew words, a particular thing stood out of the Hebrew that carried the concept for me. It translated as "guardian." A guardian has the care of a person or the property of another. He covers something that belongs to someone else. The point is this: whoever you are covering belongs to God. Embracing this concept will keep you from possessing or owning or "lording it over" somebody else. Even though a pastor covers his congregation, the people belong to God. If that is true, why do we need a covering? Why do we need a pastor?

Titus 1:5 – For this reason I left you in Crete, that you would set in order what remains and appoint elders in every city as I directed you,…

Acts 20:28 – When they had appointed elders for them in every church, having prayed with fasting, they commended them to the Lord in whom they had believed.

These Scriptures are referring to elders in the church. I am citing them to guide our concept of a pastor because pastor literally translates as shepherd, and we clearly see from Scripture that elders "shepherd" the church of God. Certainly we can draw our definition and principles about pastors from the practice of those leaders that the Bible said should shepherd the church of God.

To be in order a church needs elders.

To set the church in order. Paul left Titus on the island of Crete to appoint elders in every church. Doing this would set things in order. The Greek wording here means "to set further to rights" and "to correct in addition." When the church has leaders that take care of and shepherd the members of the congregation, it brings order to the body and things function properly. Paul and the party of people who were traveling with him in ministry made sure that they appointed elders in every church. This was the normal process that the apostles used to set churches in order. To be in order a church needs elders; it needs pastors who shepherd the church.

I want to line out three of my presuppositions here, and ask you, the reader, to please grant me these givens. Scripture supports these lines; that's why I'm laying them down for you.

*Titus 1:5-7 – For this reason I left you in Crete, that you would set in order what remains and appoint **elders** in every city as I directed you, namely, if any man is above reproach, the husband of one wife, having children who believe, not accused if dissipation or rebellion. For the **overseer** must be above reproach as God's steward, not self-willed, not quick-tempered, not addicted to wine, not pugnacious, not fond of sordid gain, but hospitable, loving what is good, sensible, just, devout, self-controlled, holding fast the faithful word which is accordance with the teaching, so that he will be able both to exhort in sound doctrine and to refute those who contradict.*

1 – Bishops, Presbyters, Overseers and Elders are all the same. Note that in the Titus scripture Paul uses the terms elders and overseers to refer to the same leaders.

I Peter 5:1-2 – Therefore, I exhort the elders among you, as your fellow elder and witness of the sufferings of Christ, and a partaker also of the glory that is to be revealed, shepherd the flock of God among you, exercising oversight not under compulsion, but voluntarily, according to the will of God, and not for sordid gain, but with eagerness; nor yet as lording it over those allotted to your charge, but proving to be examples to the flock.

2 – Apostles, Prophets, Evangelists, Pastors and Teachers are also Elders. Peter calls himself an apostle and a fellow

elder. If an apostle is a fellow elder, all five-fold ministers are fellow elders.

3 — Elders are to be people of good character and good conduct. When you add I Timothy 3:1-13 to the above Scriptures from Titus chapter one and I Peter chapter five, it is obvious that elders are to have godly character and act in a godly way.

In the New Testament the word apostle occurs at least 21 times; prophet occurs at least 11 times; evangelist at least 3 times; pastor 1 time; teacher 6 times. It stands out that pastor occurs only once, although the Greek word, which means "shepherd," is used 6 times to refer to Jesus Christ, as the Shepherd. To help us better see what a pastor is to do, I am listing several Scriptures and changing the English word "shepherd" to "pastor." After all, it is the same Greek word.

I Peter 2:25 – For you were continually straying like sheep, but now you have returned to the **Pastor** *and Guardian of your souls.*

Ephesians 4:11 – And He gave some as apostles, and some as prophets, and some as evangelists, and some as **pastors** *and teachers,...*

I Peter 5:4 – And when the Chief **Pastor** *appears, you will receive the unfading crown of glory.*

Acts 20:28 – Be on guard for yourselves and for all the flock, among which the Holy Spirit has made you overseers, to **pastor** *the church of God which He purchased with His own blood.*

I Peter 5:2 – **pastor** *the flock of God among you, exercising oversight not under compulsion, but voluntarily, according to the will of God; and not for sordid gain, but with eagerness; nor yet as lording it over those allotted to your charge, but proving to be examples to the flock.*

From these Scriptures emerges a pretty clear picture of what a pastor is to do.

Chapter Eleven

YOUR PASTOR: WHAT DOES HE DO?

So here are our questions: What does a pastor do? What is pastoring?

*I Peter 5:2, 3 – shepherd the flock of God among you, **exercising oversight** not under compulsion, but voluntarily, according to the will of God; and not for sordid gain, but with **eagerness**; nor yet as lording it over those allotted to your charge, but **proving to be examples** to the flock.*

I like how Peter has expressed it here. Pastors are to exercise oversight with eagerness and prove to be examples to the flock. And they are not to feel compelled or go after gain and riches, or to boss people around and try to control them. I have heard more than one teacher of the Word express it this way: There are many pastors, but one Lord. Pastors are never to lord it over anyone. In the last quarter of the twentieth century the Shepherding Movement was strongly taught and practiced in charismatic circles. There were some abuses, where leaders tried to compel their followers and lord it over them. Years ago, I attended a meeting of many of the shepherding movement pastors in the Seattle area, and one particular situation left a bad taste in my mouth. A regional pastor of some prominence came into the conference room. He was followed by one of his disciples. That disciple carried the pastor's brief case, stayed behind him a few steps, and in general, acted like a lackey. And that pastor just seemed to let it happen, basically ignoring his brief case-carrying disciple. I didn't speak to either man, so it might not have been what I thought it was. But the "vibe" I got made me hesitate. While shepherding was a Biblical concept, could it be that some of these shepherding leaders were taking it too far, and erring in the area of being bigger bosses, and allowing their followers to relate to them in a "master – servant" way? It gave me pause, and allowed the Lord to guide me to carefully consider the shepherding doctrine and how it was being practiced.

What does a pastor do? A good pastor never lords it over the people that God has entrusted to his care. Pastors are to exercise oversight with eagerness and prove to be examples to the flock.

Acts 20:28-31 – **Be on guard** *for yourselves and for all the flock, among which the Holy Spirit has made you overseers, to* **shepherd** *the church of God which He purchased with His own blood. I know that after my departure savage wolves will come in among you, not sparing the flock; and from among your own selves men will arise speaking perverse things, to draw away the disciples after them. Therefore* **be on the alert**, *remembering that night and day for a period of three years I did not cease to admonish each one with tears.*

A pastor is to be on guard for his flock. He is to be on the alert and protect them from wolves and from people who would try to hurt the body of Christ. A number of years ago I was pastoring a small church in Vancouver, Washington. In one Sunday morning service, I had a woman stand up in the service to share a testimony. At first it sounded good and encouraging, giving thanks to the Lord, but then the tone changed, and she began speaking accusations against another local pastor. I immediately stopped her and had her sit down. I did it in firmness, but as gently and lovingly as I could. I cited the Scripture that states clearly we are not to receive an accusation against an elder except on the basis of two or three witnesses (I Timothy 5:19). As the pastor of the flock, it was absolutely clear to me that she needed to be stopped. I was on guard and alert, and I took the correct action, in firmness and love. After the service I had a brief meeting with a couple of the younger elders in the church, and they were wondering why I had seated the lady. They expressed that her testimony sounded good and encouraging to them, and they didn't understand what the problem was. I took the time to read Scripture with them, and to exhort them to listen more carefully and to be on the alert and to guard the flock of God. They received it well. I bring this up to illustrate that a pastor needs to see things at whatever higher level the Holy Spirit will help him with, so that the flock is guarded and protected.

What does a pastor do? A good pastor will guard his flock and keep on the alert so that individuals who might hurt the people of the church will be recognized and thwarted in their attempts to do damage.

Titus 1:9 – (the overseer must be) **holding fast** *the faithful word which is in accordance with the teaching, so that he will be able both to* **exhort** *in sound doctrine and to* **refute** *those who contradict.*

James 3:1 – Let not many of you become **teachers**, *my brethren, knowing that as such we will incur a stricter judgment.*

A good pastor knows the Bible and sticks firmly to it. He is able to warn people of dangers by speaking sound doctrine. He is able to stand up and correct or refute those who speak God's Word incorrectly. He teaches the Word, even though he knows that God will hold him to a higher standard because of it. He better do it right.

I met a strong man of God back in 1980, and he eventually became my father in the Lord. He was ordained as an apostle, and had the strongest teaching ministry I had ever encountered. There are many leaders in the Lord who have taught me and helped equip me to be a good pastor, but none as much as Apostle Dick Benjamin. I had taken Hermeneutics (principles of interpretation) in Bible College, but still saw many people interpret God's Word in such a way that two could totally disagree over one Scripture. Dick taught, emphasized and practiced one key principle, and it has helped me to be a careful teacher of the truth. That principle? Scripture interprets Scripture. Whatever the topic, a true teacher will examine every verse that relates to the topic: whether it is in the paragraph, or the particular book of the Bible, or the Testament it is in. Only by examining all the verses can you begin to uncover the full counsel of God.

What does a pastor do? He handles the Word of God in such a careful and accurate way that he can easily exhort, refute and teach his flock the word of truth.

*I Timothy 5:17 – The elders who **rule well** are to be considered worthy of double honor, especially those who work hard at **preaching and teaching.***

A good pastor knows how to rule well.

A good pastor knows how to rule well. I emphasize this because I have seen that leaders can be correct, even in their interpretation of Scripture, but be wrong because of the way in which they communicate to people and manage their fellow leaders and congregation. I am presently an elder in a new church in McKinney, Texas. Mike Connaway is my pastor, and as I have watched him work with me and with other leaders of people and ministries within the church, I have marveled at how well he relates to other leaders. He is a master of "the principle of being over and being among." He is the Senior Pastor, and that gives him the dominant vote and leadership in everything that has to do with the church. But he does not have his fingers wrapped around every ministry and every action in the church. He is not a micro-manager. In my twenty years of experience in the business world, I saw time and time again that many managers did not know how to manage their own managers, foreman, lead men, etc. They were so involved in micro-managing that people could not become all they were capable of. They had not learned how to rule well. Pastor Mike has a relaxed hand with the congregational leaders under his oversight. He has men like me, who have pastored for many years and have some experience and wisdom, as well as young men who have little experience, but tremendous levels of enthusiasm. He listens to them all, evaluates their ideas and insights and offers wise counsel when needed. But almost always it is like a team decision: he is among us. Rarely does he have to assert his will and decision over someone else: rarely over us. He communicates, listens and allows other people to minister and to lead. That's what ruling well is all about.

What does a pastor do? He rules well; he knows how to lead the leaders in his church, without dictating, over-controlling or over-ruling. He knows how to listen to his ministry leaders, to ask good questions and to give wise counsel as needed. People have their gifts and ministries recognized and developed. He really is the coach of the local church team.

As you and I consider how to connect to our pastor, it is important that we know what a pastor is and what he does. Seeing that character and ministry in our pastor will firm up our relationship and give us resolve in making the pastoral connection. To review what a pastor does:

1. Protection. He is on guard for us, and he is on the alert. This is overall care and defense. We may never know about someone who is a threat to us, but he knows and takes action against them, in order to protect us. He keeps watch over our souls. This is individual care and communication, given to encourage, edify, exhort and comfort us.

2. Instruction. He labors in teaching and preaching, handling accurately the word of truth given to us in Scripture, and holding fast the faithful word established by our apostles and prophets.

3. Direction. He has charge over us in the Lord, and exercises oversight in a careful, loving manner. He rules well over everyone in the congregation, followers and leaders, without dictating to anyone, or lording it over them.

4. Correction. He exhorts (warns and instructs) everyone with sound doctrine, correcting error as needed, and refuting those who would contradict and try to further bad doctrine and practices that could hurt the congregation.

5. Example. He proves to be an example of a disciple of Jesus. He practices what he preaches, and we can follow Him, as He is following Christ.

Our Holy Spirit Legend takes this shape: What is the will of the Holy Spirit? He raises up leaders for every church to have a pastor. And He does something special: He equips your pastor to do a great job shepherding you; He holds your pastor in His right hand (Revelation 1:16), to give him special help and to hold him accountable. He wants you to put yourself into connecting and relating to your pastor. Do what it takes to receive and enjoy the benefits of his ministry to you. The Holy Spirit says, "Your pastor is an under-shepherd to you; place yourself under his ministry and embrace the benefits of being led and shepherded by him. Follow him as he follows Christ!"

Our catechism for connecting with our pastor is first about the pastor:

Catechism

Question:
What is my Pastor?

Answer:
He is my covering and guardian. He gives me protection, instruction, direction and correction. He proves to be an example for me.

Chapter Twelve

YOUR PASTOR: WHAT DO YOU DO?

Every one of us, new and old, needs to be connected to our pastor. He is our covering. We have established what our pastor is to be in character and conduct. He gives us protection, instruction, direction and correction. He proves to be an example for us.

We have also established how each one of us is to be a connected member of our local church. We need to connect with people and use our gifts and ministry to build the body of Christ. That being said, let's examine how we are to relate, communicate and connect to our pastor. I am addressing the subject that pastors do not like to talk about. In fact, most pastors won't talk about how the people in their congregation should conduct themselves toward the pastor: it's too controversial and often not received by church people. But you and I need to hear it. Let's look at what our character and conduct should be toward our pastor.

I Thessalonians 5:12, 13 – But we request of you, brethren, that you **appreciate** *those who diligently labor among you, and have charge over you in the Lord and give you instruction, and that you* **esteem them very highly in love** *because of their work. Live in peace with one another.*

We need to appreciate our pastor, and esteem him highly in love because of the work he does for the Lord and for us.

Back in the 80's I was pastoring a church in Vancouver, Washington. A young single lady from one of our family churches near Sacramento had an internship at Hewlett-Packard, and we opened our home for her to stay during the summer. She appreciated being able to stay with us, and was a faithful member of our church during that time. But over the weeks she grew more and more distant and dissatisfied with me. When my wife and I sat down with her, to find out what was wrong, and what could be done to improve things, she finally expressed the problem. <u>I was a pastor and I watched too much T.V.</u> Now over the years there were times that we watched a lot of T.V in my family; other times we got rid of the television for months at a time. At the time she stayed with us, we were watching several hours of television each week. But my wife and I were puzzled that this could be such a problem to her. She had an idea of what a pastor should be doing in his home, and it didn't include television. In her mind she had put me (and all pastors) on a very high pedestal, and when my television watching removed me from the pedestal she couldn't accept that. I point this out to say simply: there is a difference between having high regard for our pastor and putting him on a pedestal. No Christian leader can last for long on a pedestal that we have erected.

To appreciate our pastor literally means to know him. This doesn't mean that the pastor is to be our best friend and spend personal time with us. Just think about it: in a congregation of 300, how could a pastor find enough time and soul to be "best friends" with everyone in the congregation? Over the years I have seen many times that people leave a church because the senior pastor doesn't spend as much time with them as they want. That's very unrealistic. But we can know him in the sense of knowing and caring all about him. I am part of a new congregation in Texas. The church is growing in size (about 300 now). I know all about my pastor in the sense that I know about him and care deeply for him. Once in a while my wife and I have lunch with Pastor and his wife; mainly to see how they are doing and find out what he would like us to be doing. But I really get to know about him by listening to his sermons. He shares real life stories from the life of his family and the church, and I learn so many things about him. Just by listening to his sermons I know him more and more. The more I know about him, the more I see how much he labors in his ministry among the members of the congregation. Seeing his work and seeing his family leads me into more of what God wants me to do in relating and connecting to him.

How do we connect to our pastor? We need to know about them: their work, their labor, their family, their life. Then we need to esteem them (honor and look up to) with love.

Hebrews 13:7 – Remember those who led you, who spoke the word of God to you; and considering the result of their conduct, imitate their faith.

Many years ago there was an ordained teacher who had a strong teaching ministry and was gaining reputation throughout the region because of his systematic instruction in God's Word. But there was a problem. His teenage children were wild. People knew about their inappropriate conduct, and he did not keep them in the discipline and instruction of the Lord. Things came to a head when his teenage son fathered an illegitimate child with one of the girls in the youth group. He continued teaching and preaching, doing the best that he could. But his ministry suffered because people couldn't see past the sinful conduct of his children. There's a reason that Scripture specifies that an elder needs to have children who believe and cannot be accused of dissipation or rebellion (Titus 1:6). You see, in determining how we relate to our pastor, we need to consider the results of his conduct; and if the results are good, we are to imitate them. But if the results are not good, then we have no example to imitate.

How do we connect to our pastor? We remember his life and we consider the results of his conduct. When the results are good, with faith and love, we imitate him.

Hebrews 13:17 – Obey your leaders and submit to them, for they keep watch over your souls as those who will give an account. Let them do this with joy and not with grief, for this would be unprofitable for you.

Oh boy! Here it comes. I'm going to talk about submission and obedience. People don't want to hear it. The 21st century church has become so independent-minded that church leadership fears addressing the Bible teachings of submitting to and obeying our leaders. But it's Bible and every new and old Christian must practice these Bible concepts to connect with their pastor. It's key to the Alpha Omega Paradigm.

"You ain't the boss of me!"

In our times, the way that all people relate to authority has deteriorated to the point that it's merely a weak whisper of how it should sound. How children relate to their parents, how students relate to their teachers, how children on the bus relate to the bus driver, how young people relate to police, how employees relate to their bosses; there is almost no submission, and very little obedience. As a result parents, teachers, bus drivers, police and bosses rarely exercise their leadership and authority as they should. They have grief and they fear leading like they should. I could sum it up in one phrase: "You ain't the boss of me!"

The truth of God's Word is that we are to obey our pastor. In the rare times when he needs to tell us what to do, we need to listen and do it. Sometimes he knows best in the Lord, and he needs to be able to speak to us freely. He shouldn't be compromised by fear of our rejection of his words. He needs to know that he has the freedom to speak into our lives. Are we willing to allow that? We need to submit to him. That means to place ourselves under his authority. We need to trust that God is powerful enough to keep our pastor in line, and correct or remove him if it is needed. Our pastor has to give an account to the Lord Jesus Christ of how he has shepherded those that God gives him to care for. He will stand before His master, Jesus, and be judged for his leadership conduct. You and I must trust God and show our attitude and actions of obedience and submission.

Let me address one more question that might come up. What if my church is a really big church, with thousands of people in the congregation? How can my pastor have this relationship with all the people and me; and how can all the people and I have this relationship with him? Well, most large churches have leadership structures that include other staff pastors and/or elders that can develop the close areas of knowledge and relationship. Avail yourself of that relational path in your church, with your leadership. But remember, your senior pastor and you still have the responsibility to fulfill the over encompassing concepts of pastoral leading and church member following. Do it in the excellent way that the Lord Jesus Christ desires for you. Even if there are tens of thousands of people in your church, you can still know, love and respect your Senior Pastor. And he will fulfill his pastoral responsibilities toward you in love and servant-hood.

How do we connect to our pastor? We communicate with a heart and life of obedience and submission to his leadership, and we do it in such a way that he has joy in his heart; never grief.

Now let's embrace our catechism:

Catechism

Question: How do I connect to my pastor?

Answer:
I will consider the result of my pastor's conduct.
I will obey and submit to my pastor in the Lord. I will highly esteem my pastor in love. I will trust and appreciate my pastor.
I will aspire to bring my pastor joy, not grief.

Part Five

Talking with God

Precept #4:
Connect to God in Prayer

Chapter Thirteen

PRIVATE PRAYER

Let's review a bit of our Alpha Omega Paradigm.

Revelation 1:8 – "I am the Alpha and the Omega," says the Lord God, "who is and who was and who is to come, the Almighty."

The phrase "who is and who was and who is to come" is a clear expression of the timeless eternal nature and presence of God. It is the New Testament way of expressing the Old Testament memorial name of God: Jehovah (I Am). Jesus Christ is the great I Am, and illustrates it again within His Alpha Omega statements.

Revelation 21:6 – Then He said to me, "It is done. I am the Alpha and the Omega, the beginning and the end. I will give to the one who thirsts from the spring of the water of life without cost."

Combining the phrases "It is done," and "I will give to the one who thirsts from the spring of the water of life without cost," establishes clearly that the whole Alpha Omega Paradigm must first be based upon the salvation point. Jesus Christ can only be the Alpha and Omega because He died on the cross to enable any and every man to have everlasting life. And Jesus Christ can only be our Alpha Omega if we accept our salvation by grace through faith. We must have that point in time where we say something like this, "Jesus, I accept you as my Lord and Savior. Forgive my sins and come into my heart and rule my life." From that moment on it all works!

Our next paradigm line is about connecting to God in prayer. It is crucial that we talk with God, and our private way of doing it will spell success for our Christian life. We have gotten away from our prayer roots, as established in the first century church, and as taught by Jesus Christ Himself. Over the last 1500 years the leadership of the church has made prayer too much of a formal and liturgical function. Prayers were to be offered at churches in special services and using special words and forms. Prayer became something that was hard work, and sadly, part of the "works" of righteousness that Christians needed to perform to receive forgiveness for their sins. The sad thing about this is that individual Christians, for the most part, allowed this to happen without holding fast to the personal, tender and intimate thing that prayer was meant to be. It is because individuals have found it easier to practice being unaware of Jesus Christ within them; and if one is unaware of God within, why pray, except on the rare occasions that one tries to be aware of God's presence?

But God's design for prayer is that we connect to God quickly, simply and continuously. This is a crucial precept in connecting with God in the strong, life-long pattern of the Alpha Omega Paradigm. He wants to have simple, clear and concise conversations with each one of us.

Matthew 6:5-8 — When you pray, you are not to be like the hypocrites; for they love to stand and pray in the synagogues and on the street corners so that they may be seen by men. Truly I say to you, they have their reward in full. But you, when you pray, go into your inner room, close your door and pray to your Father who is in secret, and your Father who sees what is done in secret will reward you. And when you are praying, do not use meaningless repetition as the Gentiles do, for they suppose that they will be heard for their many words. So do not be like them; for your Father knows what you need before you ask Him. Pray then in this way: Our Father who is in heaven, Hallowed be Your name. Your kingdom come, Your will be done; on earth as it is in heaven....

In Jesus' time hypocrites made a practice of "so called" praying in public. They would find key places on the street corners, or at the front of the congregation in synagogue. They spoke loudly, projecting their voices to be heard by everyone. The Greek word here for hypocrite means "actor." That's why I said their practice was "so called" prayer. If prayer was to be words between an individual and God, these hypocrites weren't saying anything for God to hear. Jesus pointed out that they did it to be seen by men. Is that what prayer is to be about?

Now the Gentiles had a different way of praying. Jesus said they used meaningless repetitions, and went for long prayers with many, many words. They repeated the same words and the same phrases over and over again, like chanting. Or they used hundreds and hundreds of words; long treatises of complicated phrases that nobody could follow or understand. God is not into chanting, and He does not like lofty oratory. They were not connecting with God in conversation. Instead they had man-made, religious ideas, and there was no communication going on with God. Jesus pointed out that they supposed they would be heard. Is that what prayer is all about?

Private Prayer

Let me state here that corporate prayer is a Bible-based doctrine that is important and necessary in the church. Jesus is the one that brought us the "two or three" principle. He encourages us to gather together, two or three (or more), and assures us that He will be present in our midst in a special way. He also promises that whatever the group will ask He will grant, to the glory of the Father. Corporate prayer is much needed, but private prayer is a prerequisite to the development of any and all kinds of prayer.

Jesus, first of all, wanted to establish that the most important aspect of prayer is to be private. He used three phrases to drive his point home: your inner room, close the door, and pray to your Father who is in secret. If you and I pray in private, one-on-one with God, He will reward us. We need to pray in secret, one-on-one with Jesus, talking about anything and everything. Back in the 70's and 80's, a popular format emerged within the church for teaching. As certain key teaching leaders came up with important subjects for the greater Body of Christ, they would put together 8-12 hours of instruction, and have a week-end seminar. In a Friday night and a full Saturday the teaching was well presented and received. One such seminar that I was blessed to be able to attend in Bellevue, Washington, was about having an established prayer closet. Four decades later I no longer have my notes from that seminar. But one key thing remains vivid in my memory and in my prayer life. The speaker had one page in his seminar notebook that simply had two words in large bold print: "Prayer Closet." He exhorted each and every one of us to find one place in our homes or offices, where we could go, shut the door and talk with God. At the time I was attending Bible College and lived off campus in a small apartment with my wife and first daughter. There seemed to be no place that could work for my prayer closet. What I finally found is that the water heater closet had a little extra space. I could set up a folding chair in that closet. It was awkward to climb over it and sit down, but I could (just barely) and close the door. If I was careful I could avoid banging my knees. Once I was inside, in the dark, I could calmly talk with God. That helped me develop the life pattern of personal, private talks with Jesus. I now do it many times daily; there's no more water "prayer" closet, but I do it several time each day. Jesus wants me talking to him in private.

We need to re-think our use of the Lord's Prayer.

In our private prayer we need to develop straightforward talk. We should pray with simple and truthful words. Jesus presents what we have traditionally called, "The Lord's Prayer," as an example of prayer that is not repetitious, meaningless or overly wordy. Let's just think about that for a minute. In the church the Lord's Prayer has become a repeated "exact words" prayer that congregations speak again and again and again. How many millions of times do you think this repetitious prayer has been spoken over the years? What Jesus meant to be an example of private, secret and simple prayer, we have turned into a repetitious form and ritual. We need to re-think our use of the Lord's Prayer.

Let me sum up the emphasis of the Lord's words. God is who He is and has done what He has done. Know that and acknowledge that as part of your talking with Him. That's what He wants.

I want to insert a parenthetical thought here. I am a Pentecostal and have many years experience as a pastor in Pentecostal and charismatic churches. If you do not believe that the gift of tongues is for the church today, you might want to skip the next few paragraphs. I believe that speaking in tongues is a legitimate gift of the Spirit and should be practiced in the life of those who have been baptized with the Holy Spirit. That being said I have found far too many examples of Christians speaking in tongues in a way that doesn't edify the whole church, and in fact is Biblically out of order. So let me say this: your private prayer is the place for you to practice speaking in tongues.

I Corinthians 14:18 – I thank God, I speak in tongues more than you all; however, in the church I desire to speak five words with my mind so that I may instruct others also, rather than ten thousand words in a tongue.

In the Corinthian church there were a lot of Christians who exercised the gifts of the Spirit, especially the gift of speaking in tongues. There was imbalance in the congregation that Paul wanted to correct with his instruction. He teaches in I Corinthians chapter fourteen that in the church services tongues that are spoken should be interpreted, so that all may be edified. But in concluding that teaching he says that he speaks in tongues more than all the Corinthians did. The Biblical teachings that direct decency, order and edification in the church services are great, balanced doctrine that many Pentecostals and charismatics should learn from. So I ask the question: when did Paul speak in tongues? The obvious answer is that he did it in his private prayer time. That's the place for praying in tongues. According to Scripture you are speaking mysteries when you speak in tongues, and that act of speaking in tongues edifies you. To build yourself up, speak in tongues often and sincerely in your private prayer time. It's good for you!

Chapter Fourteen

RIGHTEOUS PRAYER

We sometimes feel that we must be "qualified" in order to have correct and effective prayer. It is true that we must be qualified. But it is not true that we have to qualify ourselves. This addresses the crux of what our "righteous prayer" is.

James 5:16 – The effective prayer of a righteous man (person) can accomplish much.

A recent speaker in our church referred to this Scripture to emphasize our holiness, and how we needed to prepare our hearts, lives and conduct, so that we approach God in prayer from a position of righteousness. **Fallacy:** We need to get righteous, repent and do right works to have effective prayer.

John 9:31 – We know that God does not hear sinners; but if anyone is God-fearing, and does His will, He hears him.

This Scripture has been incorrectly interpreted by many. Let's look at the context. One Sabbath day Jesus crossed the path of a man who was born blind. The disciples assumed that the reason this man was born blind was because somebody had sinned. They asked, "Who sinned that this man is blind: was it him or his parents?" Jesus removed the sin issue completely by declaring that the blind condition was to be for the glory of God. Then He healed him in an unusual way. He made mud, put it in his eyes and told him to go and wash in the Pool of Siloam. The blind man did just that and he was healed! This was great, but the Pharisees did not like it. They were already against Jesus, and opposed anyone who supported Him. So they called the man born blind to be in front of them and asked him what happened. He told about his healing, and they then asked him what He thought about this Jesus. He responded, "He is a prophet." They didn't like that answer, so they called the blind man's parents, and tried to put them on the spot. Now they knew that the Pharisees were going to excommunicate anybody who supported Jesus, so they side-stepped the issue: "This is our son, who was born blind, and he now can see, but we don't know how it happened. Ask him; he's old enough to answer for himself." So once again the Pharisees called the man born blind and put him on the spot. They were trying to get him to acknowledge that the healing must not have come from Jesus. They themselves said that they did not know where Jesus came from. At this point the healed man got somewhat sarcastic with them: "Well isn't that interesting? We know that God does not hear sinners, and yet God must have heard Jesus because he healed me." They rejected what he said and kicked him out of the synagogue. There was no way they could acknowledge Jesus as the Christ. Now I am telling you the whole story because you need to see two things about the statement: "We know that God does not hear sinners." Firstly Jesus did not say this; the blind man said it. Secondly he was only repeating what the religious people of that day believed: the Pharisees were the ones who taught that God would not hear sinners. But because some people don't consider all the context of John chapter nine, they think it is a true concept from God. **Fallacy:** God won't hear our prayers if we sin.

Luke 18:13 – But the tax collector, standing some distance away, was even unwilling to lift up his eyes to heaven, but was beating his breast, saying, 'God, be merciful to me, the sinner!' I tell you, this man went to his house justified rather than the other; for everyone who exalts himself will be humbled, but he who humbles himself will be exalted."

If God did not hear sinners, he would never hear any of us. All have sinned and fall short of the glory of God, but God does hear sinners. **Truth:** Because of His love and mercy, God does hear sinners.

Luke 23:42, 43 – And he was saying, "Jesus, remember me when You come in Your kingdom!" And He said to him, "Truly I say to you, today you shall be with Me in Paradise."

This is what one of the thieves on the cross said to Jesus, as they were being crucified. For this man on the cross, or for you and me when we accepted Jesus into our hearts and lives, God did hear us even though we were sinners. **Truth:** Because of His love and mercy, God instantly hears sinners and answers them.

James 5:17, 18 – Elijah was a man with a nature like ours, and he prayed earnestly that it would not rain, and it did not rain on the earth for three years and six months. Then he prayed again, and the sky poured rain and the earth produced its fruit.

I'm all alone in serving You, and I just want to die.

Earlier we touched briefly on the previous verse (16) which says that the effective prayer of a righteous man can accomplish much. We know that it wasn't talking about our own righteousness or righteous works, because Elijah is then pointed out as an example of effective prayer. It says that Elijah had a nature like ours. What is that talking about? Elijah was a prophet used fantastically by God in prophecy, prayer and miracles. He had prophesied that drought was coming on the land, and it did. Then after three years he was ready to confront the prophets of Baal. He challenged them to a duel: whoever (Jehovah or Baal) sent fire from heaven and consumed the sacrifice, he would be called the true God. The prophets of Baal danced and cried all day, even cutting themselves with knives. But Baal didn't answer. Elijah taunted them, even saying that maybe Baal was stuck in the outhouse! When it came Elijah's turn, he dug a ditch around the altar, filled it with water, poured water all over the sacrifice on the altar, and then prayed for Jehovah to take the sacrifice. He did, sending fire from heaven that consumed the sacrifice, even licking up all the water in the surrounding ditch! The people watching then declared: "Jehovah, He is God!" Elijah told the people to kill the prophets of Baal, which they did. It was at this point that he prayed for rain, three times, and the rain came, a mighty deluge. Then in the power of God's Spirit he outran the king's chariot in going back to Jerusalem. Great prophecy, great prayer, great miracles. But let's keep following the story. When Elijah got back to Jerusalem, the ungodly queen was upset about her prophets of Baal being killed, and she declared that she was going to have him killed. In great fear Elijah fled into the wilderness. God miraculously provided water and "super-strength" food for him. In the strength of that food he traveled for many days to the mountain of God. God asks him what he is doing, and Elijah puts on the big whine: "Everything is going wrong, and I am all alone in serving You, and I just want to die." He then experiences mighty earthquakes and storms as God asks again what he was doing. And again Elijah whines: "Everything is going wrong, and I'm all alone in serving You, and I just want to die." God responded by giving Elijah his next assignments, which included anointing his replacement! And he reminded Elijah that there were still quite a few left in the land who did not bow the knee to Baal. Now I told that story because I want you to see that Elijah was a man with a nature like ours. He had strengths and he had weaknesses. He did right things and he committed sins. The point you need to see is that Elijah was not cited as an example of what a righteous man is. He was cited as an example of a regular man, like you and I, who could put strength and effort into his prayer. **Truth:** Elijah is not an example of righteous works, but of human nature, with all its weakness & sins.

So what about a righteous man? What about righteous prayer? What constitutes a righteous person?

Romans 3:10 – As it is written, There is none righteous, not even one;

Dilemma – If no one is righteous, how can there be a righteous man; how can there be a righteous prayer? Who can pray and get results?

II Corinthians 5:21 – He made Him who knew no sin to be sin on our behalf, so that we might become the righteousness of God in Him.

Solution – We are righteous humans because we are in Christ Jesus. I am a righteous man; you are a righteous person; because we have the righteousness of Jesus Christ, we are considered righteous by God! We are the ones who can pray, as righteous individuals, and have much accomplished by that prayer. Now some people cite certain Scriptures to try and prove that if we commit sins after we are saved, we must do something before we are again forgiven, and can then have our prayers answered. Maybe we have to confess; maybe we have to perform acts of contrition, but we have to do something in order to be righteous again. But that puts us right back into earning our righteousness, and we can't do that.

Psalm 66:18 – If I regard wickedness (iniquity) in my heart, the Lord will not hear;

This verse is sometimes cited to support the idea that if we sin, God won't hear us. But this is not talking about a Christian who stumbles and sins. It's talking about someone who has regard for wickedness/iniquity in their heart. That means they think about it, build it up, and allow it to rule their heart. That's a lot different than stumbling and sinning. Even when a Christian commits sin, God still hears him. Jesus Christ died on the cross to pay the penalty for all of our sins: past, present and future. **Fallacy** – If I commit a sin, the Lord will not hear me.

I John 1:9 – If we confess our sins, He is faithful and righteous to forgive us our sins and to cleanse us from all unrighteousness.

Church doctrines and practices have been built around the requirement that Christians confess their sins. It has led to an incorrect default idea: if we don't confess our sins, then God won't forgive us; God doesn't forgive our sins until we confess them. It ends up being a "works" doctrine: the work of confession that is needed before we are forgiven. That's just not true. The blood that Jesus shed on the cross paid the penalty for all of our sins: past, present and future. As a Christian, if I did something with the money in the checkbook, and didn't want to tell my wife what I had done, so I lied to her, that would be a sin. If I was killed before I had a chance to confess and repent, would I still go to heaven? Absolutely, yes! My sins, including that lie were covered and forgiven when I accepted Jesus Christ as my Savior and Lord. To better understand what I John 1:9 is referring to, one needs to look at the context of the chapter. It becomes obvious that it is talking about our hearts and minds at the point when we become a Christian, not at the time after we are Christians and we commit a sin. Before we were Christians, we might have thought or said that we have no sin or haven't committed any sin. But at the point that we accept Jesus Christ as Savior and Lord, we are confessing our sins, and He both forgives us and cleanses us from all unrighteousness at that moment. That is what 1 John 1:9 is referring to, and that's the beauty of our salvation. Don't fall into a fallacy that adds "works" to your salvation. **Fallacy** – If I commit a sin, I am not righteous again until I confess that sin.

You and I need to understand, accept and embrace our position in the Lord Jesus Christ. We need to say: I am a righteous person. I am a righteous person! I am a righteous person!! In accepting that we begin to see that we are just like Elijah in nature and we can be just like Elijah in effective, fervent prayer. We need to say: I am Elijah. I have the nature of Elijah. I come in the Spirit of Elijah. I come in the power of Elijah. I am Elijah!

We can pray the righteous prayer because we are righteous individuals in Christ Jesus. So let's put our minds and hearts into our prayers and we will see much accomplished! That's what righteous prayer is all about.

Chapter Fifteen

CONSTANT PRAYER: IT'S CONVERSATION

So how does the prayer thing really work? How formal? How mystical? How religious? How often? How complex? Jesus walked this earth as a common man. He wasn't a country yokel, but He could talk in a regular way, in the regular language of the common people. He could speak the most profound truths in simple, straight forward ways. His illustrations gripped the hearts of all people because they could identify with Him. He was fully man, tempted in all ways just like every human, yet without sin. He could relate to the lofty Pharisees, the despised tax collectors, the lowest publicans and sinners. He didn't change after He died and was resurrected. He is the same Jesus. How do you want to talk to your "regular guy" Savior?

Conversational Prayer

*Philippians 4:6 – Be anxious for nothing, but in everything by **prayer** and **supplication** with **thanksgiving** let your **requests** be made known to God.*

*Ephesians 6:18 – With all prayer and **petition** pray at all times **in the Spirit**, and with this in view, be on the alert with all **perseverance** and **petition** for all the saints, and pray on my behalf, that utterance may be given to me in the opening of my mouth, to make known with boldness the mystery of the gospel,..*

Conversation is talking. Note the many synonyms and phrases used for prayer in these verses: prayer, supplication, thanksgiving, requests, petitions, in the Spirit, perseverance. In order to do any or all of these things you have to talk. Quit making prayer some "mystical" or "holy" form of communication. Prayer is conversation. It is talking. God is your friend; He is inside of you, and He wants so much to have talks with you. Quit mystifying Him and embrace the talks!

Conversation is listening. Listen to yourself pray. Listen to other people pray. Ask yourself: Why is almost all of our prayer us doing the talking?

Revelation 2, 3 – He who has an ear, let him hear what the Spirit says to the churches.

Matthew 11:15 – He who has ears to hear, let him hear.

I Samuel 3:10 – And Samuel said, "Speak for Your servant is listening."

We tend to be impatient in our talks with God. We thank God for what He has done, we talk about our life and problems, we let our requests be made known, and then what? It's not that God doesn't also talk. It's more that we haven't learned to listen. Jesus emphasized how important it was that we take the time to hear him. When young Samuel was instructed on how to respond to God calling him, it was simple: let God know that you want Him to speak, and that you are willing to listen.

A couple of times each year Jan and I drive down to the Houston area. It is about a four hour drive. During that time we choose to converse; to have conversation. We talk back and forth. There are times that it is quiet between us, but we actually have a real talk about the trip, our lives, our family, etc. She talks, I listen. I talk, she listens. It's O.K. if silent pauses happen. I'm willing to wait to hear her, and vice-versa. That's what conversation is: speaking and listening on the part of both parties.

I'm an old married guy (46 years) so I talked with one of the single men in our church to get an idea of how singles handle it when they really want to have a talk with someone. For him the most common thing was to go to Starbucks together, and spend time sipping and talking; talking and sipping. Even though it is a public place, people ignore the hustle and bustle and noise around them, and put effort and focus into talking and listening. That's good conversation.

During this past year (2015) we had record rainfall in Texas. Even though our church building is on a slight hill, the basement had some serious flooding. We're talking about thousands of gallons of water coming in: all day and all night for several days. It meant that the pastor and his family, as well as many members of the congregation spent hours and hours with wet vacs, buckets, mops, brooms, pumps, etc.; taking out gallon after gallon of water in order to keep the floors and walls from being damaged. It turned into a great bonding time as people served, shoulder to shoulder in caring for the facilities. And a lot of talking went on. People learned new things about one another. It was great conversation: far beyond the typical "How are you doing," and "I'm doing fine," that passes for conversation on a Sunday morning. People talked and people listened: great, meaningful conversation.

Prayer is talking with God. It is one-on-one conversation with God. You should talk, and listen. God does talk, and listen. In our talks God does want to talk, as well as listen. We need to listen, as well as talk. If we can have conversation with other people that includes talking and listening, then we can have listening and talking in our prayer with God.

Constant Prayer

*I Thessalonians 5:17, 18 – pray **without ceasing**; in everything give thanks; for this is God's will for you in Christ Jesus.*

*Ephesians 6:18 – With all prayer & **petition** pray at all times **in the Spirit**,...*

Pray without ceasing; pray at all times in the Spirit. All times? Without ceasing?? Did God really intend to put this kind of "prayer burden" upon us? It seems to me that this is the quickest way that we condemn ourselves in prayer life. Some people rise up early in the morning to pray. But for others of us, we can't seem to do that. We barely get up early enough to scramble out the door and rush to work. Then we feel guilty that we didn't pray early in the morning. We hear of how Christ wanted His disciples to pray with Him for one hour in the Garden of Gethsemane, and they failed. We try to pray for a long time, but can't seem to make it past 15 minutes. Then we feel guilty that we couldn't pray for one hour. We're gathered together with the family, and we are asked to say grace before the meal. We stumble through some words, but it's not long and eloquent. Then we feel guilty that we couldn't pray the eloquent grace prayer for the meal. We commit to praying more each day, but get caught up in everything going on, and as we go to sleep at the end of the day, we realize that we didn't pray much at all. Then we feel guilty that we couldn't even remember to pray. We hear about mighty prayer warriors that spent so much time on their knees that they had huge, misshapen calluses on their knees. We kneel down to pray, and after a few minutes it hurts so much that we get up and relax in the recliner. Then we feel guilty that our physical comfort is more important to us than prayer. Our pastor asks us to sign up for an hour during the upcoming 24-hour Prayer Burn. We sign up, show up for our hour, and find ourselves thinking about other things at work or at home, instead of praying. Then we feel guilty that we can't seem to keep focused on praying. We read about prayer without ceasing, and we can't even imagine praying non-stop. We hear about another Christian who is spending time in prayer and we feel guilty because we aren't doing the same. Guilty, guilty, guilty. What in the world is wrong with us?

All of this is false guilt. It comes from the one who condemns us. It is the tune that he keeps playing to accuse Christians of failing. His aim is to get us to quit because of condemnation. He is Satan, the accuser of the brethren, and he seeks to steal and to kill and to destroy. What does God want? He wants to talk with us. He wants to hear from us. He wants to share with us. What will we do to bring that about? Let's refocus.

Now here's the important part: we are in each other's presence the whole time.

It is not about what we constantly do. It is about what God is always doing and about where God is, always. Look back at the conversational prayer example I used about my wife and I driving to Houston. For about four hours, each way, we have the opportunity to talk and to listen, back and forth. Is there talk going on, non-stop, for the full four hours? Of course not. Sometimes the radio is playing; sometimes the focus is on the traffic around us; sometimes one or both of us is thinking about something else; sometimes there is just silence. Now here's the important part: we are in each other's presence the whole time. Even if talk is not going on, both of us are present. The good thing is that we do talk and listen a lot during the time, as needed. Now let's think about the reality of "presence." God is always present within us; 24-7-365. At any moment, and in every moment, we can talk with Him. Granted, we sometimes forget that He is there, but that doesn't mean He's gone. And we are always present within us; 24-7-365. Let's take the focus off of constant prayer, and instead put it on constant presence. Since He is constantly present within you and I, and you and I are constantly present within ourselves, then at anytime we can pause and talk with Jesus; at anytime we can pause and listen to Jesus. It may be 15 seconds here, 30 seconds there; a few minutes at another time. That is prayer without ceasing, because of the constant presence of ourselves and God. Practice His constant presence because He is constantly present. There's no guilt in that; there is constant opportunity.

Let's connect to God in prayer. For private prayer, let's make a prayer closet to use in increasing our secret, private prayer life. In conversational prayer, it's just talking and listening, so let's do more of it with Jesus. We can start out: "Hello, Jesus." With righteous prayer, let's see ourselves as we really are: we are Christians and each of us is a righteous person, so we can pray with effort, intensity and fervency. And we will get results and accomplish much. By practicing the constant presence of God, we can constantly talk with Him. His presence guarantees our access!

Our Holy Spirit legend comes out like this: What is the will of the Holy Spirit? He draws each one of us to accept Jesus as our Savior and Lord, and then to embrace that we have the righteousness of Jesus Christ, and we are righteous individuals, who are qualified to ask Jesus for anything. He is helping us de-formalize prayer, de-bunk the false and lofty ideas of what prayer is to be, and come down to earth to talk with Him; just to have conversation with Him as our informal and intimate friend. He wants us to talk, talk, talk with Him. He wants to have conversation at any time, in any moment. He wants us to listen and learn to hear Him. He is saying, "How's it going? Tell me what's on your mind, what's working for you, what's not; don't be afraid to express your thoughts and feelings to Me; I want to hear you talk, and I want to respond to you." That's divine conversation!

On to the catechism:

Catechism

Question: What is prayer?

Answer:
Prayer is conversation: talking with God.

Part Six

Our Only Objective Standard of Truth

Precept #5:
Connect to God's Word

Chapter Sixteen

GOD BREATHES THE SCRIPTURE

The Bible is God's Word. Why is that so important? We need an objective standard of truth. That means it is truth that does not change. It is not influenced by any human's opinion. Over the years humans change in what they believe; what is moral or immoral; what is true or false. They can't seem to stick with any one truth; they change opinions based on what they want, what they think the majority wants, what they think is socially important, what they think the voting public wants or what will make them the most money. If you want a current example, just look at the last ten years and ask yourself: what is marriage? It wasn't that long ago that Congress passed the Defense of Marriage Act, which defined marriage as between one man and one woman. But in 2015 we saw the president of the United States change his opinion and say that marriage could be between two women or two men. This was the same president who declared that marriage was only between one man and one woman when he was first running for election. Not long after his announcement the U.S. Supreme Court decided that marriage was not limited to one man and one woman, but could be between two women or two men. It struck down state laws across America, regardless of what the citizens of those states wanted. Our laws are not an objective standard of truth: they will change over time because man changes. But God does not change; He knows everything and He knows what is right and what is best. We need to have a solid connection with God's Word from the newest to the oldest Christian. The Bible will keep us solid and grounded in the way we walk our abundant Christian life and successfully perform the work of the ministry that leads to His kingdom and His righteousness being established. So what is His Word and how do we work with it? How can we even understand it?

Scripture is Breathed by God

II Timothy 3:16, 17 – All Scripture is inspired by God and profitable for teaching, for reproof, for correction, for training in righteousness, so that the man of God may be adequate, equipped for every good work.

II Peter 1:20, 21 – But know this first of all, that no prophecy of Scripture is a matter of one's own interpretation, for no prophecy was ever made by an act of human will, but men moved by the Holy Spirit spoke from God.

All Scripture is inspired by God. Inspired literally means "breathed by." It is good for us (profitable) because our teaching, reproof, correction and training come from it. No Scripture comes from human interpretation or human will because the Holy Spirit moved the men who spoke it and wrote it.

Jewish leaders through the years have linked these words:
Torah - Talmud - Targums.

---

1 — Scripture is breathed by God. For the Jewish people they highly revered the first five books of the Old Testament. They called this group of books the **Torah**. In our Bibles we title these books Genesis, Exodus, Leviticus, Numbers and Deuteronomy. They were authored by Moses; we refer to them as The Law. The function of the synagogue in the time of Christ was primarily to review, memorize and instruct in the Torah. Let me introduce you to two more "T" words: Talmud and Targums. For every part of the Law, Jewish leaders through the years have linked these words: **Torah - Talmud - Targums.** Now here's where the difficulty comes in. Some Jewish rabbis place an equal value on all three. And that shouldn't be. You see, the Torah is God's Word; Moses wrote it, as the Holy Spirit guided him in what to write. The Talmud is commentary, written by men about the Torah. It is very good; after all, men have written many very good books. But it was not inspired by God. And the Targums are like sermons: very good sermons that try to explain and illustrate both the Torah and the Talmud. But once again, like sermons, the Targums are composed by men; sometimes very good, but not inspired by God. You can't look to the Talmud and the Targums to be free of error. In the same way, the commentaries and sermons that are available to us are helpful, but are not the standard of truth. We need God's Word to be our objective standard of truth and guidance.

Torah and Bible = God's Word, inspired, infallible, unchanging and without error

Talmud and Bible commentaries = Man's word about God's Word, written by men, fallible, with errors and subject to change.

Targums and Bible sermons = Man's opinion about God's Word, spoken by men, fallible, with errors and subject to change.

In a similar way we need to be careful when using Bible translation and paraphrases. What is God's infallible Word, and what is man's interpretation? When we are looking at a good translation of the Bible we need to find one that sticks to telling us what the Word says, without trying to add words that tell us what it means. What it says is equal to translation; what it means is interpretation (like commentary). When you really want to know what the Bible says, when you want to know what is "breathed by God," find a really good translation. I like the New American Standard Bible myself.

2 — Scripture is not influenced by the human authors. Their opinions or desires did not affect the Bible book(s) they wrote in any way, shape or form. Now how can I say that? We don't believe that God just grabbed their brains and vocal chords and turned them into automatons. And if you have read any of Paul's epistles, he does express his opinions on more than one occasion. So here's the deal. The Holy Spirit was so involved that only the words that were God's opinions and God's desires got into the Bible books. If it was a man's opinion, it was only allowed to get through the screen of the Holy Spirit if it was also God's opinion or desire. Because of this, we can never say about any part of the Bible: "That's just one man's opinion." This is the reason that people who don't want to agree with or accept something in the Bible must first reject the doctrine that all Scripture is breathed by God. If you do not believe that God breathed the Bible, then you can dismiss whatever parts of it that you want to, by relegating it to some individual person's opinions, desires or prejudices.

People, who do not believe that the Bible is God's Word, choose to believe instead that different men authored the different books. That allows them to commend the Bible, but not be morally bound to it. After all, they will say that whatever those authors had in their minds and hearts affected what they wrote. So their political views, personal desires, or petty prejudices came through in the books that they wrote. They may have been really good people, but no matter how good their intentions, sin, selfishness and even wickedness put socially unacceptable things in the Bible. If we accept that, then we will have no objective standard of truth, and our view of right and wrong will sway with the winds of humanity.

Why did God do it this way? He knew that no human could present the truth as it is needed by man. He knows all about our opinions, strategies, plans and schemes. He also knows about our sin. He knew that any "scripture" or "standard" that we came up with would not stand the test of time; it would not serve our need to have an objective standard of truth. Man's approach to needing an objective moral standard is simple: we don't think we need one. Just look at the Constitution of the United States. It has a process by which it may be amended or changed. It's because we somehow think that morals must change through the years because we change what we want to do and what we don't want other people to do. And we have to have nine judges tell us what the Constitution means because some people change their opinions quicker than others do. And as those nine judges change, even their group opinions change. Suddenly the Constitution doesn't mean what it used to mean. Face it: we need our moral and perfect God to give us a written guide that never changes, but remains our needed guide.

3—Scripture has no errors. Skeptics just love to find "seeming errors" in the Bible so that they don't need to be accountable to its truths. I'm not going to address those seeming errors, except to say this: In 48+ years of being a Christian, there has been no seeming error or contradiction that I have found, or that someone has pointed out to me, which could not be explained or resolved. If you have encountered some error or contradiction that you can't understand or explain, I encourage you to seek out your pastor, or someone you respect with regard to their walk in Christ, and let their input help you to see that Scripture has no errors.

It is important that we have Scripture without error, so that it can be our objective standard. Our salvation takes a step of faith. Our belief in God being perfect and holy is also a step of faith. If the Bible is God's Word, and it contains errors, then God makes mistakes. I can't go down a road like that. Our God is perfect, His Word is without error, and we have the standard of truth that we all need.

4 — Scripture equips us for everything good that we can and will do. Our life in the Lord is all about seeking His kingdom and His righteousness. As we do that we see more clearly the work of the ministry that He wants us to do. The Bible is profitable; that means it makes a good return. As we use it, we are taught and trained in righteousness. It provides for us whatever reproof or correction that we need. God wants each of us to do every good thing that is needed for our Christian life to be brisk and lively; an abundant life. I'm not talking about us having to do good works. But God wants us to partake of the best possible abundant life that we can have. His Word is given, not to saddle us with works we have to do, but to help us have a full and wonderful life.

Chapter Seventeen

GOD OPENS OUR MINDS AND EXPLAINS THE SCRIPTURES

If you consider all of our colleges and universities, you quickly realize that we value knowledge and study. Think of all those term papers that students have written. Think of all the doctoral theses that have been written and then orally defended in front of committees. We seem to have mastered the art of study, and we're proud of our scholarship. Look at all those fancy robes, banners and ribbons at the graduation ceremonies. But handling the Holy Scripture is a different task. Many times individuals, such as you and I, have pondered over Bible verses and have not been able to figure it out. It seems to be beyond our grasp. If we just depend upon the study and wisdom of man, we resign ourselves to criticizing and demeaning the Scriptures. Since we're so smart and scholarly, the problem must be with the Bible. "There must be something wrong with the Bible, because I just can't explain what this part means." That's why we have to have divine help.

God Opens Our Minds to Understand the Scripture

Luke 24:44-47 – Now He said to them, "These are My words which I spoke to you while I was still with you, that all things which were written about Me in the Law of Moses and the Prophets and the Psalms must be fulfilled." Then **He opened their minds to understand the Scriptures,** *and He said to them, "Thus it is written that the Christ would suffer and rise again from the dead the third day, and that repentance for forgiveness of sins would be proclaimed in His name to all the nations, beginning from Jerusalem.*

In Luke chapter 24 we are told the story of Jesus appearing to the eleven apostles plus others. This was after He had been crucified, died and rose from the dead. The women who followed Jesus had gone to His tomb to put perfume and spices on His dead body, but His body was not there! Angels appeared to them and announced His resurrection. The women went back to the others, where the eleven apostles and several others were gathered. They told them what had happened; Peter ran to look into the tomb and saw no body. These disciples of Christ wondered in amazement and awe: what is going on? Two of them took a day trip to Emmaus, and encountered Jesus along the path and in their home. They were so excited that they ran back to Jerusalem to report the appearance to the Eleven. At that moment Jesus suddenly appeared in their midst. They were amazed and frightened; He assured them that it was really Him. "Look at my hands and my feet." They were so overcome by their emotions that they didn't know what to believe. He took a piece of fish from them and ate it in front of them, to help convince them that He was really there. Get the picture here: Jesus had been telling them that He was going to be killed in Jerusalem, and that He would rise again after three days. On His final night with them, He re-iterated this. When the angels talked to the women at the tomb, they repeated the death and resurrection truth again, and the women repeated it to the whole group. The two men who went to Emmaus were told this basic story of resurrection victory again, and they had run back to the others and repeated it to them. Then

Jesus appeared to the whole group! They're still having trouble wrapping their mind around the reality of the resurrection of Jesus. What finally happened to bring them over the hump of unbelief? He opened their minds to understand the Scripture. Regardless of what their close friends told them, regardless of what they experienced, it still took Jesus to open their minds to understand the Scriptures. Only then were they able to make the leap of faith and embrace Him. Two things:

Man's efforts. Human skills, thoughts, knowledge, expertise, efforts or experience cannot bring understanding of the Scriptures. I attended Bible college and was taught all about Scripture, from Genesis to Revelation. I learned Biblical Greek, so that I could read and understand the New Testament in its original written language. I studied the systematic theology of famous Christian leaders, from Martin Luther to Charles Finney. I developed a reputation within the church of being a "theologian." I made it my quest to be a teacher and defender of apostolic doctrine. But I have come to this basic position: no matter how smart I am, no matter how sharp my teachers were, without God's help I cannot grasp and understand the truth of Scripture. It is not like reading some book written by men. It's much deeper than Shakespeare's plays; it is fuller than any set of encyclopedias; it's much more profound than the thickest dictionary. Man, by himself, cannot fully understand the truth of Scripture.

God's help. Thanks be to God through our Lord Jesus Christ. Only God can open our minds (our intellect) to understand the Scriptures. We need to accept that the Bible is unlike any book ever written by man through the ages. His Word is above our intellect. If we are really going to understand it, we have to have His help. That's the beauty of it: He is willing and able to help, and He opens our minds to understand the Scriptures, if we ask Him to help.

God explains to us what the Scripture means

Luke 24:27 – Then beginning with Moses and with all the prophets, He explained to them the things concerning Himself in all the Scriptures.

Were not our hearts burning within us.

Luke 24:32 – They said to one another, "Were not our hearts burning within us while He was speaking to us on the road, while He was explaining the Scriptures to us?"

Looking again at the post-resurrection appearances of Christ, the women had seen the empty tomb, heard the pronouncement of the angels that Jesus was raised, and reported it to the group of disciples that had gathered. Peter then went to the tomb to find it empty. All the disciples were marveling at this. Two of them (one was Cleopas) took off on a seven mile walking trip to Emmaus. They were talking back and forth about the empty tomb events. Jesus came up and began walking with them (they were prevented from recognizing Him). He asked, "What are you guys talking about?" They responded, "Haven't you heard about the big happenings in Jerusalem? If you haven't heard, you're about the only one." Jesus again asked, innocently, "What happenings?" They responded that Jesus, a mighty prophet had been arrested and killed by crucifixion. They had hoped that He was going to redeem and restore Israel, but He was killed. Now it had been three days and some women visited His tomb, found it empty, and had a vision from angels saying that Jesus was alive. Others had also seen the empty tomb.

Let's pause in telling the story. The way Cleopas told the story showed a lack of understanding, a lack of faith, and a lack of acceptance of what Jesus had been telling His disciples for quite some time before He was crucified. First, Cleopas called Jesus a great prophet. Yet Jesus had made it clear to His disciples that He was much more than a prophet; He was in fact, God. Second, Cleopas presented the absence of the body of Jesus from the tomb on the third day as a mystery. Jesus had stated clearly to His disciples that He would be crucified, but would rise again on the third day. Third, Cleopas expressed the limited view about Jesus that the disciples had clung to for so long: that Jesus was there to restore the earthly kingdom of Israel. Jesus had expressed to His disciples in a number of ways that He was not on the earth to restore the nation Israel, but to build His Father's heavenly kingdom and bring salvation to all mankind. It seemed that the group following Jesus was set in their ways and thinking, and just couldn't seem to get away from their own desires and preconceived ideas.

At this point Jesus took over the discussion in a strong way: "You foolish guys! Your own emotions and thoughts have made you slow to believe what you needed to believe!" He then proceeded to go through the Scriptures from the Law and the Prophets to explain everything concerning Himself. When they came close to Emmaus, He made as though He was going on, but they urged Him to stay with them, so He agreed. As they reclined at table to eat, He took the bread, broke it and blessed it. Immediately they recognized Him: it was Jesus! And He disappeared! They rushed back to Jerusalem to tell the disciples what happened.

The two verses above bring the most important aspects of this story to our attention. It took Jesus going through the Scriptures from the Law and Prophets, explaining the things concerning Himself, for them to gain understanding. And while Jesus was doing that it impacted their hearts, their very souls, their thoughts, feelings and desires. Their hearts were burning! That's something we can relate to. There's nothing like the feeling when one is looking over some particular part of the Bible, and suddenly the Holy Spirit explains it to us in a simple and clear way. We feel like God has given us a special revelation and it feels great! There's nothing like that feeling: it's deep, it's spiritual, it's significant, it's important. Don't you just love it? But why do we need God's explanation? We're pretty smart, after all.

Scrambling. Our understanding gets fogged and scrambled by our own motives, desires and pre-conceptions. Let's call it our premises, presumptions. The disciples of Jesus seemed to have tunnel vision when it came to His mission. They wanted Him to restore Israel: kick the Romans out, get rid of the Gentiles and restore Israel. They were so focused upon that desire that they couldn't understand what Jesus told them again and again: "I'm going to die for the sins of the world and provide salvation." At one point Peter even took Jesus to the side and rebuked Him for talking about dying. His spiritual mission just didn't fit into their desires and preconceptions.

De-fogging. God has to defog our fog, unscramble our scrambling, and clear our stuff out of the way so we can really understand the Scriptures. We can't do it ourselves, and we can't do it for each other. If we try, it results in more convoluted fog and scrambling. We must have God's help.

We can help. Our thoughts and feelings won't help. But our desires, if pointed properly, do help. Our desires come from our volition, our will. We can help clear the fog and scrambling by wanting only what He wants. Not my will, but Thy will be done. This is a true surrendering of what we want, about when things happen, about where things happen, about how things happen. In the old days, back when I was a teenager, we sang songs about that, as we tearfully fell to our knees at the altar. "I Surrender All," and "I'll go where you want me to go, dear Lord," were two that remain vividly in my mind. Too often our desires attempt to dictate to God what His will is to be. Think about it. Are you willing to do what God says to do, at the moment He wants you to do it? While you are willing to minister for Jesus, are you willing to do it wherever He wants you to do it? If you know what you are supposed to do, and have a plan for how you're going to do it, are you willing to do it the way God wants it done? Will you be willing to do as Gideon did, and send almost all of the army home, pick up pitchers and lanterns, and go to the camp of the enemy? It sure wasn't Gideon's plan, but he did it the way God told him, and it worked! The submission of our will to His will puts us in the right frame of mind and soul for Jesus to explain to us what the Scripture means. He defogs us, unscrambles us and explains what the Scriptures mean.

Chapter Eighteen

THE HOLY SPIRIT GUIDES AS SCRIPTURE INTERPRETS SCRIPTURE

When Jesus walked the earth with His disciples, He was a Helper (Greek-Paraklatos) to them. He explained the Scriptures by applying them to real life. When He died on the cross, was resurrected and finally ascended into heaven, He specified that the Holy Spirit was another Helper, and He would continue the process of helping them to understand the Scripture by guiding and teaching.

The Holy Spirit Guides and Teaches Us In All Scripture

John 14:26 – But the Helper, the Holy Spirit, whom the Father will send in My name, He will teach you all things, and bring to your remembrance all that I said to you.

John 16:13 – But when He, the Spirit of truth, comes, He will guide you into all the truth; for He will not speak on His own initiative, but whatever He hears, He will speak; and He will disclose to you what is to come.

Holy Spirit action. God inside of us, the Holy Spirit, is the precious gift God gives us, to guide us by the Scripture, to teach us from the Scripture and to sharpen our memory of the Scripture.

But here's the problem: our individual soul and spirit are also inside of us.

I have a relative who is a pastor. On our last vacation we had an opportunity to visit with his family. We enjoy a wonderful fellowship because we are fellow believers in the Lord Jesus Christ. There was something heavy on his heart. The leaders of his small denomination were going to consider the issue of gay marriage, and he was concerned that the decision might go in favor of accepting gay's lifestyles and gay marriage. In his denomination they have a strong belief and doctrine about the "Inner light" that every believer has. They are strongly guided by their inner light. The doctrine is that the Holy Spirit is inside of them, and will guide them as their inner light. It is true that the Holy Spirit is inside of every Christian believer, and He is perfect and knows the right thing to do in everything. But here's the problem: our individual soul and spirit are also inside of us. And guess what? We are not perfect and we don't know the right thing to do in everything. That's why we must have the Bible as our objective standard of truth. God has also designed the church in such a way that we can be guarded from our own imperfection and lack of knowledge of the right thing to do. It is why we have other Christian believers around us; it is why we have our pastor; it is why we have covering in the body of Christ. If we are obviously wrong, we can receive correction; if we are sincerely wrong, we can be directed in the Scriptural ways of the Lord.

But if we decide that our "inner light" is right, no matter what, we may be making the mistake of saying something is of the Holy Spirit when it is of ourselves.

Having said that, when we are reading and studying the Bible, the Holy Spirit guides and teaches us by the Scripture and from the Scripture. With the safeguard of our church, our pastor and the Bible, we can rejoice in the ministry of the Holy Spirit to us.

Holy Spirit coverage. His action is high, good and powerful, to such a degree that we have everything we need from the Scripture, for every time, every place and every situation. He teaches "all" things, and guides us into "all" the truth. I will say this, teach this and shout it from the hills throughout my life: we should not limit the application of the "all" ministry of the Holy Spirit. From the prisoner of war who is shut away from the church and the Bible for years, to the church member who is right in the middle of a church scandal with a fallen pastor, the Holy Spirit is there, as perfect teacher and guide, with the Bible, which is God's Word without error, to cover "all" situations and "every" need.

Scripture Interprets Scripture

II Timothy 2:15 – Be diligent to present yourself approved to God as a workman who does not need to be ashamed, accurately handling the word of truth.

The Bible is our objective standard of truth, given by God to guide us into abundant life, as we move forward in the work of the ministry for Him and His kingdom. It is wonderful that He explains His Word to us and opens our minds to understand. In that we have a responsibility to handle His word in the best possible ways.

Our handling of Scripture must be pure. When we approach His Word, our premises must be untainted by our thoughts, ambitions, etc. Remember the disciples of Christ? Their dogged determination that the kingdom was to be restored to Israel was their premise. It had been taught to them by religious authorities who had the same dogged dedication to this obsession with getting rid of the Romans and having their own country. This all ended up tainting and twisting what the disciples heard from Jesus and how they interpreted the Scriptures. Jesus eventually got them straightened out. We need to set aside premises and approach the Scripture with a pure heart. Our motives must also be pure. Scripture is not our piggy bank or magic wand. Every time we approach God's Word we need to purify our hearts. What I like to say is this: "Lord, it is all You and only You that I want to be honored and affected by Your Scripture in my life. Help me, Lord to be pure as I handle Your Word."

Our handling of Scripture must be diligent. His Word is wonderful and it does so much for us. But it is not to be handled lightly. In this day and age, it is easy to attend our Sunday morning service and hear a weekly sermon, and think that's sufficient. Here's the difficulty: God does not intend that we get spoon-fed a little Word here and a little Word there. He truly wants us to love and treasure His Word. God promises that people from all nations and people groups are going to come into the church in the last days. They will be looking for something specific: to be taught God's ways and how to walk in God's paths. We want to be diligent in handling God's Word, so that we can teach them what they want and need. Brothers and sisters, we need to put some effort into handling Scripture so that we can do the work of the ministry for all those people God is bringing into His church.

Our handling of Scripture must be accurate. The most valuable thing that my father in the Lord taught me was that "Scripture interprets Scripture." The simplest way for me to describe this is with the word "context." Every Scripture needs to have the context considered in order to see God's true meaning. Look at the paragraph the verse is in. Look at the chapter it is in. Look at the particular book it is in. Look at the covenant it is in: Old Testament? New Testament? Look at the rest of the Scriptures that address the topic. I was always refreshed by how my father in the Lord approached any subject. He would begin by reading approximately twenty passages of Scripture. He would do this because He had looked at <u>every</u> verse in the Bible that contained the topic, and he boiled it down to the ones that were most relevant and would help his audience to understand the topic. That was Bible teaching; that was consideration of the context; that was accurately handling God's Word of Truth. This manner of handling God's Word also should warn us off of what I like to call "finger magic." It is the idea that you get guidance from God by flipping the Bible open and blindly sticking your finger down to find God's guidance for you in the situations of life. That is not how to walk in the paths of the Lord. That's wishful and lazy thinking. Come on, God's far above and beyond that kind of thing. No finger magic; instead handle the Bible accurately.

Let's connect to the Bible. Remember, Scripture is special; God breathed it just for us. He is so concerned that we understand it, that He supernaturally opens our minds to understand it. He is personally involved with His Word, so He takes the time to explain it to us. His Spirit guides and teaches us in the Scriptures and because of all that, it is vital (life giving) that we handle it carefully because Scripture interprets Scripture. I hope you are beginning to see that all these Alpha Omega Paradigm premises are inextricably linked.

Your connection to God inside of you is strengthened by your connection to His Bible. Your connection to your church and to your pastor gives you safeguards that keep you from error in your interpretation and application of the Bible. Your connection to God in prayer enables you to have free access to the guidance of His Spirit. It all is intertwined. The better one connection is the better all the connections are.

The Holy Spirit legend for the Bible: What is the will of the Holy Spirit? The Holy Spirit is teaching us what the Scripture says and means; He is guiding us into everything by helping us see the applicable Bible verses; He is recalling to our memory whatever Scripture we have read, studied or memorized. He wants us to love the Bible, to handle it carefully and to learn the ways of the Lord from it. That way we can teach all the people who come into the church, seeking how to walk in the ways of the Lord. He is saying: I am the Breath (Spirit) of God and I have breathed the Bible for you. Love it, treasure it, read it, study it, and let Me be your guide to the truth."

Now let's visit our catechism:

Catechism

Question: What is the Bible?

Answer:
The Word of God, breathed by Him, containing no errors, and our only objective standard of truth.

Part Seven

Appropriating the Power of Almighty God

Precept #6: Connect to God's Power

Chapter Nineteen

JEHOVAH AND EL SHADDAI: GOD'S NATURE

Revelation 1:8 – "I am the Alpha and the Omega," says the Lord God, "who is and who was and who is to come, the Almighty."

In the first Alpha Omega statement from the Lord Jesus Christ, He describes Himself with these additional words, "who is and who was and who is to come, the Almighty." In this concise statement He embodies the dual aspect of God's nature that has been emphasized from the time of the patriarchs all the way into the New Testament church age. Through the ages it seems that we have had trouble maintaining a strong equal emphasis upon both aspects, so it is clear as to why Jesus would embody both in His Alpha Omega verses.

Who is and who was and who is to come. This is an obvious statement of God's eternal presence and existence; past, present and future. In the Old Testament this aspect of God's nature came through in His formal name: Jehovah. When God called Moses to take on the responsibility of leading the Israelites out of their Egyptian captivity, he was hesitant to do it. During the long conversation with God, Moses asked Him what His name was. "If they ask me what Your name is, what shall I tell them?" God responded, "I Am that I Am. Tell them, "I Am has sent you." The Hebrew word here is a verb of being that expresses all tenses: past, present and future. It has been translated as Jehovah, although the correct pronunciation of the word is not certain. Remember also that while Jesus was on the earth, He made this statement to the Jews: "Before Abraham was born, I Am." The Jews recognized immediately that He was claiming to be Jehovah, so they took up stones to kill him for blasphemy. Jesus was Jehovah, and in this Alpha Omega passage, He emphasizes His "Jehovah" nature.

The Almighty – This is a direct reference to the Hebrew term, "El Shaddai," God Almighty, from the Old Testament. In the times of the patriarchs God did make Himself known at special times with His power and might; El Shaddai. 78% of the occurrences of El Shaddai come in the patriarchal books of Genesis and Job (Genesis-6 times, Job-31 times, the rest of the Old Testament books-10 times).

Exodus 6:2,3 – God spoke further to Moses and said to him, "I am Jehovah; and I appeared to Abraham, Isaac, and Jacob, as El Shaddai, but by My name, Jehovah, I did not make Myself known to them.

God makes an interesting and important distinction in His discussion with Moses. He indicates that with the patriarchs He had appeared to them as El Shaddai, which translates God Almighty. But He did not make Himself known to them by His name, Jehovah. People have taken this to mean that the patriarchs did not know or use the name Jehovah. If we look back in Genesis we see that they did know the name Jehovah.

Genesis 4:26b – Then men began to call upon the name of the LORD (Jehovah).

Genesis 17:1 – Now when Abram was ninety-nine years old, the LORD (Jehovah) appeared to Abram and said to him, "I am God Almighty (El Shaddai); walk before Me, and be blameless."

Genesis 26:24 – (Isaac at Beersheba). The LORD (Jehovah) appeared to him the same night and said, "I am the God of your father Abraham;...

Genesis 28:13 – (when Jacob had the dream of the ladder up to heaven, with angels ascending and descending on it). *And behold, the LORD* (Jehovah) *stood above it and said, "I am the LORD* (Jehovah), *the God of your father Abraham and the God of Isaac;...*

Jehovah spoke to Abraham, He spoke to Isaac and He spoke to Jacob, specifically speaking His name (Jehovah) to Jacob. And before the patriarchs the Scripture indicates that men began calling on the name of Jehovah. So what did God mean in Exodus 6:2, 3? The patriarchs knew and used the name Jehovah, but they related to God as El Shaddai. How did that work?

El Shaddai expresses God's nature of power and might in action.

Their relationship to God orbited around His power expressed in what I like to call "might events." El Shaddai expresses God's nature of power and might in action. The patriarchs related to God, event by event.

Event: God appeared to Abram, identified Himself as El Shaddai (God Almighty); then He announced the coming birth of Isaac, changed Abram's name to Abraham and instituted the circumcision sign of the covenant (Genesis 17:1).

Event: When Isaac was sending his son Jacob away to escape the death threats of Esau, and to get a wife from Laban's relatives, he knew that Jacob needed special protection. His parting statement to Jacob: "May El Shaddai (God Almighty) bless you." (Genesis 28:3).

Event: When God appeared to Jacob at Bethel He identified Himself as El Shaddai (God Almighty) and changed Jacob's name to Israel (Genesis 35:11; 48:3).

Event: When Jacob faced the unusual situation in which one of his sons was a captive in Egypt, and the only way they could get more food from Egypt was to have the rest of his sons take his youngest son Benjamin with them for the Egyptian official to see (this was the secret plot Joseph was playing on his brothers); Jacob feared that he would lose his only remaining special son, and he spoke his desperate hope: "May El Shaddai (God Almighty) grant that the Egyptian official will have compassion..." (Genesis 43:14).

The patriarchs didn't relate to God as someone that was always around (Jehovah). They saw Him as coming and going; sometimes with them and sometimes not. They wanted Him to be there for certain events. They saw Him as the God of might and power for special times: El Shaddai. God recognized this weakness in His people. Since they didn't relate to Him as Jehovah (ever present God), it was easy for them to fall into the trap of acknowledging and serving other gods.

God knew there had to be a change in how the Israelites viewed Him. With Moses and the Israelites, moving forward from Egypt, they needed to be brought back into balance: they needed to know and experience that God was present with them all the time. In Egypt, in the areas of their sojourn trip and even in the Promised Land, people had all kinds of gods. They had many gods. People changed who their god was, depending upon how their present circumstances were going. If they lost the battle, they would switch to their enemy's god. If the harvest failed, they would switch gods. If they didn't like how their life circumstances were going, they would switch gods. It was almost like our modern proverb: they would switch gods as often as they changed their socks! God wanted His people to stick with Him, no matter what. He was establishing a new covenant (the Mosaic Covenant) with them, and it would be based on them sticking with Him, no matter what. That's why we see the emphasis in the first of the Ten Commandments:

Exodus 20:2 – I am the LORD (Jehovah) *your God, who brought you out of the land of Egypt, out of the house of slavery. You shall have no other gods before Me.*

So we see these dual aspects of the nature of God. God wants both to be strong and fully embraced by His people. Jehovah shows the timeless eternal nature and presence of God: God is always there with you. El Shaddai shows God's nature of power and might in action: God expresses His power and might every time it is needed (need event). God's people must practice embracing both aspects all the time. Don't misunderstand me. I don't mean we need to have a 50-50 view and practice. It needs to be 100-100: relate to our Lord Jesus Christ full blast as our Jehovah and our El Shaddai; His presence and His power.

Through the ages there has been a progression, which is sometimes good, but most of the time it has not been balanced.

During the time of the Patriarchs, they embraced God's powerful actions on their behalf, but had no problem with having other gods. Just look at how often the wives of the patriarchs had the idols of false gods. When they wanted El Shaddai to do something on their behalf, they would put away the idols, long enough to get some favor. When Abraham bargained with God over whether Sodom and Gomorrah would be destroyed, God was there. But when Abraham was done with the conversation, in Abraham's mind they parted company.

During the time of Moses, Joshua and the elders, the Israelites embraced both God's presence and His power, and it worked. God emphasized His name, Jehovah, and it brought His people right into the position they needed to be in. Granted they had some slip ups, such as the Golden Calf in the wilderness, but overall it worked correctly, and they were brought into the Promised Land with the guidance and blessing of God.

During the time after the elders and into the kingdom period, things went wrong. The Israelites drifted from Jehovah, their ever present God. Their hearts were far from Him; they built altars to other gods; they made their God just one of many gods. They still expected Him to move in power for them anytime they wanted, and they would repent, cry for help and get delivered. Then they would turn away from God again. The cycle of slide away – come back – slide away repeated again and again. That's because they practiced the El Shaddai aspect, but ignored the Jehovah aspect.

During the time of Christ and the early church, both the presence and power of God were embraced. They had God inside of each of them, and they embraced their access to the power of the Holy Spirit. Mighty miracles were the order of the day; faith in the Lord Jesus Christ burned strong; the presence of God within each individual Christian was loved and embraced.

O.K. – what about today? I have indicated that embracing both aspects of God's nature at the same time is the right thing to be doing. Two of my time examples had it right; two of them had it wrong, with neglect of the Jehovah aspect. So again, what about today? I believe we don't have it right, but we have the imbalance in the other direction; we neglect the El Shaddai aspect. We embrace salvation by faith, and we understand that God is everywhere, so we honor and accept the Jehovah aspect of our Lord Jesus Christ. But what about His power in our lives? What about His transforming power to help us overcome sin? What about His healing power to fix our hurts and heal our diseases? What about His power to make a difference in society? We want to believe in all of that, but our faith is weak. For many Christians they believe that God's miracle power stopped in the first century. For others they believe that God can heal, that He can do divinely power-ful things, but they're not sure He will. We have advanced a lot in our knowledge of everything; our doctors can perform many things that were not possible fifty years ago. We start believing that we're responsible for our own destiny. Perhaps God is with us, but expects us to handle things since we're so developed and intelligent.

Hebrews 11:6 – And without faith it is impossible to please Him, for he who comes to God must believe that He is (the Jehovah aspect) *and that He is a rewarder of those who seek Him* (the El Shaddai aspect).

This dual aspect perspective of God is well expressed in this verse. We are to absolutely believe that God exists. That's the Jehovah aspect. Beyond that we are to firmly believe that He will reward us when we come to Him. That's the El Shaddai aspect.

We have the faith for salvation. We absolutely believe that we are saved by grace and we'll go to heaven when we die. We absolutely believe that God is with us all the time; we embrace the timeless eternal nature and presence of God. But for some reason we have trouble believing that God's nature of power and might will be in action for us. Maybe we're not sure God will move. Maybe we're not sure it's God's will. Maybe we think we're supposed to do it on our own. Maybe we're weak in faith. A lot of possibilities, but the result is the same: we don't connect with the power of God like we should.

I am a disabled Viet Nam veteran. When I was nineteen, I got shot twice in my left leg, and it left permanent damage to my nerves and muscles. Over the years I have had an unusual gait (how I walk) and that has resulted in degenerative disc disease. I have had my back fused from T5 to L5, with titanium rods, brackets and screws. My wife likes to say I have a redundant Klingon spine. The back disease has resulted in nerve damage to my right leg. So I move around with a walker, and sometimes with an electric wheel chair. There is pain, almost every day, sometimes more, sometimes less. When it gets to be too much, I medicate. For forty-six years I have wanted God to supernaturally heal me. I have prayed many times and asked to be healed. I have used many different approaches to receive my healing. There have been many, many people praying for me: individuals, prayer teams, whole church congregations. Members of the church, including my wife, have had dreams and revelations from God showing me walking and moving normally, healed of my infirmities. But it has not happened. I believe I am going to be healed, but it has not happened yet. Over the years I have asked myself, "Why haven't I seen God's power to heal me? I share this because I believe that for many of us, we are experiencing the same thing. Maybe it's a need for healing; maybe it's a need for miracle finances; maybe it's a need for some other miracle; but like me, you haven't seen God's power to bring the answer. There are miracles happening in the church today. God's power is being appropriated for some. But for most of us, we have things that need God's power, and we haven't received it. That's the condition I see in the church today that represents imbalance. Somehow we are total partakers in the Jehovah nature of God (His presence), but we are not total partakers of the El Shaddai nature of God (His power). We need both, strongly; we want both, strongly. God's desire is for us to have both, strongly. We need God's nature of power and might expressed in action!

It is an Alpha Omega precept that we must get straightened out in our minds. Jesus is our Alpha and Omega. Jesus is our Almighty God. We must connect with His power. Young Christians, old Christians and every Christian in between must connect with His power.

Chapter Twenty

POWER BEYOND OURSELVES: BEYOND OUR LOVE AND THOUGHTS

Why do we want power?

God has designed His people to need His power; expressed in action for their lives. Since it is part of our Christian nature to need His power, it follows that we want it. But what is our perspective: why do we want it? There are many reasons, but the situations represented need something beyond our own capabilities. Some reasons:

1 — When circumstances are beyond our control and there's nothing we can do. Recently some of our friends from church had a court case regarding custody of their child. They had done everything they could in legal representation, depositions, official reports, etc. Now it was up to the judge to decide what would happen. It was out of their hands. There was nothing more they could do. They came to my wife and me to request prayer for God's power to move in their favor. We supported them and prayed the prayer of faith. They needed God's power to supply. There are distinct times when there's nothing more we can do. It's out of our hands, but God's power can move and we need it.

2 — When we need a miracle. Maybe it's for provision. Have you ever been out of food and groceries, and didn't know where your next meal was coming from? It's one thing when you're single; it's another thing when you're married and have little ones. You have no money; you have no breakfast for the next day. You need a miracle. Or as I mentioned earlier, about my back and legs: when the doctors have done all they can, and you need a healing. You need God's power in action.

3 — When we've done all we can. When your efforts, your strength, your knowledge, your skills just don't quite make it. Recently someone came for prayer. She was unemployed and had done all that she could in trying to find a job. Hundreds of resumes sent; many interviews; great interviews that suddenly went dead. Every time it looked like it was going to work, then…nothing. We prayed the prayer of faith with her. She needed God's hand of power to provide a job.

4 — When we want more impact from our ministry. There are times when we are being faithful to do what He wants in the work of the ministry, but we can see more is needed, or we want the ministry to multiply and increase for His glory; our motives are pure and good. We want more: more for His kingdom, more for His righteousness, more for His will, more for His glory. Maybe we don't have the skill, expertise or talent to step it up. But the touch of the Master's hand can turn any skill or talent into a Holy Spirit gift. We want the most significant and powerful ministry possible because we want to reach any and all for Jesus. We need God's hand of power.

Connecting with God's power is fundamental and crucial for every Christian. He is freely and joyfully our God Almighty. He's not El Shaddai to watch us struggle, but to manifest power in action on our behalf. Here are some insights that will help us understand His available power, approach Him to partake of His power and give us parameters for power appropriation.

Our Power Alone Won't Do It.

*II Corinthians 12:9, 10 – And He has said to me, "My grace is sufficient for you, **for power is perfected in weakness.**" Most gladly, therefore, I will rather boast about my weaknesses, so that **the power of Christ may dwell in me.** Therefore I am well content with weaknesses, with insults, with distresses, with persecutions, with difficulties, for Christ's sake; for when I am weak, then I am strong.*

We need God's additional power, in everything. We sometimes have this tendency: to do whatever it is on our own. Instead we should make sure that God touches everything we do. With His touch, whatever it is becomes supernatural; it has the Master's touch.

We are not Deists.

In the early days of our nation, there were certain people in the world, called Deists. They believed that God did create everything, but then left it all up to His creation (that's us) to handle things. It was like He went away on a very long vacation, and we were supposed to handle it from there. I mention them simply to make the point: we are not Deists.

We are not Puritans.

At the same time many of the new colonists who came to North America were Puritans. They had a firm belief in salvation by faith that only comes through the cross of Jesus Christ. But after salvation they believed that we were responsible to live life, work hard and succeed. They acknowledged and accepted the presence of God in their lives, but did not believe that He was supposed to help them in their everyday, mortal lives. There's a famous saying that comes from the Puritan philosophy: God helps those who help themselves. It's a catchy saying, but it denies the power relationship that God wants with us. We are not Puritans. The manifestation of God's power is perfected when it is expressed in conjunction with our weakness. The power of Christ dwells in us, and it's not just for us to look at admiringly, or for us to stroke and say, "Cool!" It is inside of us and available to us. When we realize that our power alone won't do it, and we need His power, then we understand and embrace that when we are weak (in ourselves) then we are strong (in His power).

Love or Sound Thinking Won't Cut it Without Power

II Timothy 1:7 – For God has not given us a spirit of timidity, but of power and love and discipline.

The spirit of fear or timidity mentioned here actually carries an overtone of chickening out. It's the opposite of being brave;

160

taking a chance; going for it. God doesn't want us to hold back. He wants us to be His kind of people that go for it.

Sometimes we think that love will answer everything. If we have love, the biggest problems, the hardest challenges can be solved and overcome. After all, Scripture teaches us that without love none of God's giftings will be valuable. There is faith, hope and love; but the greatest of these is love. The Bible is clear about that. But love alone won't cut it.

Then we think that if we can just wrap our minds around the right thoughts, the right judgment, the right truth, we can work through anything. After all, God gave us a brain to think things through, and He wants our mind to rule our emotions, so that we use sound judgment about our life and ministry. The Lord wants us to think in a way that results in sound judgment. But sound thinking and judgment alone won't cut it.

Think about it. Why can you act in love? I'm not just talking about hormones or emotion. Love is that, but it is much more: sound-thinking love and will-power love in action make love more complete. But it's even more than that. You can act in love because you know God's power is with you, in you and behind you. Think a little further. The soundest thoughts and judgments need fuel to succeed: they need God's power. Your best thoughts, fueled by God's mind, God's heart and God's power will yield supernatural results.

Love and sound thinking won't cut it without power. That is why He has given us a spirit that has all three. You have a spirit of sound judgment; with it you use a spirit of love to relate correctly to everyone as you go; and you partake of the best results because you have a spirit of power. It is the Holy Spirit that makes your spirit complete in power, love and sound thinking.

The Holy Spirit Empowers Us

*Acts 1:8 – but **you will receive power when the Holy Spirit has come upon you;** and you shall be My witnesses both in Jerusalem, and in all Judea and Samaria, and even to the remotest part of the earth.*

When it was time for the birth of the New Covenant Church, the disciples were, once again, solidly together and ready to get things going. They were ready to organize and move ahead. But Jesus knew they weren't ready, at least on their own power. So He told them to wait. He expressed two crucial things to them: 1-about their power. They would receive power when the Holy Spirit came upon them. 2-about the mission. They were to be witnesses everywhere. This action plan template is given for us to follow.

Let's look at #2 first: the mission. There are so many things that we want to do; that we need to do; that we must do. These are things in our life: our work, our family, our hobbies and so on. These are things in our church: our functions, our performances, our ministry and so on. These are things in the world: our shopping, our neighbors, our possessions and so on. There are all kinds of things we want to do, we should do and we have to do. With so many things to do, so many missions to accomplish, how do we sort it out? What are the priorities? Jesus made it very clear to His disciples: witness, witness, witness. In every aspect of our lives we want to be successful, we want to be overcomers. Satan tries to mess us up, but we have the Spirit of God within us. Every believer overcomes any confusion or opposition from Satan by the blood of the Lamb and the word of their testimony (Revelation 12:11). The blood of the Lamb is referring to our salvation through the blood Jesus shed on the cross. The word of their testimony is referring to our witness. Our life and our words are to tell the story of how each one of us came

162

to accept Jesus Christ. That's our testimony; that's our witness. In our life, in our church and in our world; in everything we do, our testimony, our witness is the mission priority.

Now let's look at #1: the power. There is so much that we try to do with our own power and effort. Maybe it's because we are confident; maybe it's because it's our practical theology of self help; maybe it's because we forget to keep in touch with Him. Jesus told His disciples to wait for the Holy Spirit, and we need to wait for the Holy Spirit. It's because He is the source of our needed divine power. His power guarantees success, victory and overcoming. It is great that the Holy Spirit is within us. It gives us security, peace and really good feelings. But He is there for so much more: power, divine power, overcoming power, Holy Spirit power! The power we so long for is available from the Holy Spirit who is within us.

Chapter Twenty-One

POWERED WEAPONS AND GIFTS TO PERFECT OUR INNER MAN

In the Physical Realm or the Spiritual Realm Our Weapons are God-Powered.

II Corinthians 10:4 – for the weapons of our warfare are not of the flesh, but divinely powerful for the destruction of fortresses.

Most of what we are doing is in the physical realm. The things of earth are part and parcel of our existence. A lot of the time we are unaware of the things happening in the spiritual realm. The Apostle Paul understood very well that everything we do is really part of the battle: a battle against the enemy of our souls, the accuser of the brethren, Satan. Focus on this particular idea. We tend to think that we must have some special kind of weapon to fight the devil; a Jedi master light sword to slash him up! But that's not what we need. Here's how it works: every time we speak the gospel of Jesus Christ, it gives the devil a body slam. Simply and clearly expressing the gospel of the Cross does a pile drive slam on any demon close by. The spoken gospel causes the devil and his demons to run away. We overcome by the gospel and our testimony about it. So for every task, every step, every ministry, every mission, our weapons are powered by God. We must use God-powered weapons. The battles we fight in both the physical realm and the spiritual realm must not rely upon our own strength, but must use God-powered weapons. Don't depend upon anything other than divinely powerful weapons!

Our Ministry Gifts Only Work According to His Power

Ephesians 3:7 – of which (the gospel) *I was made a minister, according to the gift of God's grace* **which was given to me according to the working of His power.**

I want to take our focus from the general picture of every activity in life down to the specific use of our ministry gifts to accomplish the work of the ministry. That's the real "zoom in," "focus down," "lock on target" function of our life. When addressing all of our physical needs in this world, Jesus told us to seek first His kingdom and His righteousness, and all the other stuff would be added to us (Matthew 6:33). The talents, skills and gifts that God has given us are imparted to us with the understanding that they will be used for His kingdom and His righteousness. We have been created in Christ Jesus for good works; works that God designed especially for us, so that we would walk in them (Ephesians 2:10). I like to use the phrase, "the work of the ministry." We may think our skills and talents are self-developed. Some of that is true: sometimes highly skilled individuals, such as musicians, accept Jesus Christ as their Savior and Lord. Still their skills and talents were a gift from God. And not every skill or talent is used by God for ministry. This is how it works: every talent, skill or gift that we have must be touched by God to become a ministry gift. We must take all of ourselves, including these skills and talents, and give it to the Lord. If He picks it back up and gives it to us to use in ministry, then it is a divinely powerful gift. His touch equals His empowering. We want to do the work of the ministry that He has designed for us to do. And we must use the divinely empowered ministry gifts that He gives us to perform the ministry. Only in that way can we accomplish the most that we can for His kingdom.

God's Priority Use for His Power is to Perfect Us

Colossians 1:11 – strengthened with all power, according to His glorious might, for the attaining of all steadfastness and patience;... (v. 10 - so that you will walk in a manner worthy of the Lord).

II Corinthians 3:18 – But we all, with unveiled face, beholding as in a mirror the glory of the Lord, are being transformed into the same image from glory to glory, just as from the Lord, the Spirit.

God's focus with His power is all about perfecting us. This does not contradict our previous point about God's power in the use of ministry gifts in the work of the ministry. Let me state it this way: the reason God gives us divinely empowered individual ministry gifts is to accomplish our specific work of the ministry and to build His kingdom. But all of that is used in the process of training and perfecting us to become the perfect beings that God wants us to be. That's why we can say that His glorious might strengthens (empowers) us with all kinds of dynamite power toward the end result that we develop perfect character and walk in the perfect way that honors Him.

His transfiguring power is given to us for the process of changing, "from glory to glory." I use the word transfiguring because this particular Greek word from II Corinthians 3:18 is not used very often in the New Testament. It is used in Romans 12:2 about our being transformed by the renewing of our minds to find the perfect will of God. It is also used of the time when Jesus took His three disciples up on the mount and He was transfigured before their eyes and they saw Him with Moses and Elijah. In secular Greek it was a word uniquely used to refer to one of the gods becoming a man: making the transition between the heavens and the earth. We are being taken through a divinely powered process of change, as His power brings us to perfection for Him.

So when we call upon God to be our El Shaddai, our Almighty God in power events, let's remember it is not to bring us riches, it is not to bring us fame; it is ultimately for our perfecting. Why is that so important? It is because we are being perfected to be His bride; to unite with Him at the marriage supper of the Lamb.

His Power is in our Inner Man

Ephesians 3:16-21 – that He would grant you, according to the riches of His glory, **to be strengthened with power through His Spirit in the inner man,** *so that Christ may dwell in your hearts through faith; and that you, being rooted and grounded in love, may be able to comprehend with all the saints what is the breadth and length and height and depth, and to know the love of Christ which surpasses knowledge, that you may be filled up to all the fullness of God. Now to Him who is able to do far more abundantly beyond all that we ask or think,* **according to the power that works within us,** *to Him be the glory in the church and in Christ Jesus to all generations forever and ever. Amen.*

Will the angels guide us to the power of God?

So where is the power of God and how do we access it? Is it in the heavens, where He is seated at the right hand of the Father? Is it somewhere in the spiritual realm, near the angels? Will the angels guide us to the power of God? According to this Scripture the power is inside of us. From the moment of our salvation on, God is inside of each one of us. That's why we emphasized connecting with God inside of us. Remember our first catechism:

Question: Where is God?

Answer:
Inside of me, and also everywhere.

God's desire is for us to be strengthened with power (Greek-dunamis: dynamite). That's His power. He specifies that our strengthening with His dynamite power is done through His Spirit. He then says it is to happen in our inner man: that's inside of us. Why? Because that is where His Spirit is: inside of us. He then goes on to say that the power works inside of us. Remember when we referred to the reality that our power alone would not do the task. Well, within that passage of Scripture from II Corinthians 12:9, 10 it refers to the power of

Christ dwelling in us. Reach inside, to your spirit, to His Spirit: there is where you will find His power!

I have presented a large volume of information around the power connection. But it is so important that every Christian, young, old and in between, connects to God's power.

Revelation 3:8 – 'I know your deeds. Behold, I have put before you an open door which no one can shut, because you have a little power, and have kept My word, and have not denied My name. (the church in Philadelphia).

I'm taking two concepts from the Revelation letter to the church in Philadelphia. It seems to apply to all of us, in the church today. Firstly, we have a little power: while we often seem to fall short of seeing His power manifested in us and for us, we do experience His wonderful power at salvation, and we do see unique times that He performs miracles for us: divine healing, miraculous provision, open doors where we could not open the way. We have a little power, but we need so much more. We want it to be normal and regular for us to see the hand of El Shaddai, God Almighty, moving to meet every need. Secondly, we have an open door. Our Alpha and Omega is inviting us to step through the door of "divine power access" and embrace God's El Shaddai nature of power. Embrace the Holy Spirit within you. Hold fast, cleave, and hug onto Him. Do you remember the Old Testament story of Jacob? He wrestled with God all night. When morning came, God wanted to leave, so He touched Jacob and put his thigh out of joint. I think that may mean his hip came out of joint. That had to be very painful! But Jacob refused to let go until God blessed Him. So God did bless him. We need to hold onto the Holy Spirit within us until He releases His power on our behalf!

Now, our Holy Spirit legend: What is the will of the Holy Spirit? He wants us to experience every aspect of God's nature: His presence (Jehovah) and His power in action (El Shaddai). He is dwelling securely, inside of each one of us, ever ready to give us dynamite power. He is saying, "Don't short yourself. Partake of all the power I have for you. Use it in ministry for My kingdom. Be perfected by My power. Embrace Me as I embrace you. I love you and want you as My perfect bride."

Now on to our catechism. Please notice that it sounds remarkably like our first catechism that answered the question: Where is God? It is because our place to connect to God's power is internal!

Catechism

Question: Where is God's power?

Answer:
Inside of me, and also everywhere.

IN CLOSING...WE CONTINUE

That's the beauty of the Alpha Omega Paradigm: if we are connected like we should be, our successful Christian walk continues, with abundant life in the work of the ministry. The connections continue, growing thicker and deeper. Our Alpha and Omega, the Lord Jesus Christ truly has His way, and we walk on with hope, faith and victory.

Relate to the Lord Jesus Christ inside of you. Don't first think of God in His heaven. Think first of the fullness of the Godhead inside of you. Father God is inside of you. Jesus Christ is inside of you. The Holy Spirit is inside of you. Can't figure it out? Me neither! But I accept it and I reach inside to hug Him, to love Him and to speak to Him. "Hello, Jesus!"

Love your local church as I love mine, and take your part seriously. Come together with the right people in your church so ministry function happens like it should. Don't think about how much you are a unique and big part. Instead focus on doing things that build up people around you. Stand together, in formation and order: the mighty army of God winning all battles in heaven and on earth. That's the local church in action.

Know your pastor and love him. Be aware of his life and ministry. Follow him as he follows Christ. Let him know that he has liberty in your life to speak careful, loving words of commendation and correction. Think about giving him joy as he ministers. Let obedience and submission be normal words of relationship, not words to fear or despise. Don't fear Biblical shepherding. It is, after all, what Jesus does and what He wants his pastors to do.

Talk with God. Get used to saying, "Hello, Jesus," many times throughout the day. Don't bog down with formal, fancy words. Instead talk to your regular God as the regular person you are. Develop the discipline of turning on your switch of "God awareness" many times throughout the day. When you are talking to Jesus, take the time to listen. As He says, "He who has ears to hear, let him hear what the Spirit is saying to the church." Let your heart be the heart of Samuel: "Speak, Lord; your servant is listening."

Get into the Bible. Enjoy God's divine help in reading and understanding Scripture. When you are reading and wonder what certain things are all about, ask God for the help He freely gives. By His Spirit He will open your mind to understand; He will explain things to you. He will absolutely teach you from Scripture and guide you by His Word. It will happen! Look for the times where sudden understanding comes to you from God. Enjoy the burn! It's good for you. Use it, don't abuse it. Don't play around with it, like it is some magic potion for you to scatter around. Let Scripture interpret Scripture and you will be one who accurately handles the word of truth.

Power, power, wonder working power in your God, inside of you! Practice flowing in the Jehovah nature of God (presence) and the El Shaddai nature of God (power). Don't resign yourself to a Christian existence that only has a little power. If you have a little power, praise God for it, and press into Him for more power. He will do for you far above anything that you could ask or think. He does it by the power that resides within you. The power is in you, because God has the power and He is inside of you. Love the Lord God Almighty!

I give you the Alpha Omega Paradigm as the Lord has given it to me. In all of this let Jesus be your Alpha and Omega, your first and your last, your beginning and your end, in every aspect, event and circumstance of your life and ministry.

ALPHA OMEGA PARADIGM PRECEPTS

I've used so many words to emphasize six precepts. These are the critical connections. If you have them, you will thrive in your Christian walk and the work of the ministry. If you don't have them, you will struggle in your Christian walk and your impact in the work of the ministry will be insignificant. Think about it.

Precept #1:   Connect to God inside of you

Precept #2:   Connect to your Church

Precept #3:   Connect to Your Pastor

Precept #4:   Connect to God in Prayer

Precept #5:   Connect to God's Word

Precept #6:   Connect to God's Power

CATECHISMS FOR OUR ALPHA OMEGA PARADIGM

Will you feel foolish repeating these questions and answers? Maybe. Will you benefit from repeating them, out loud? Definitely! We learn by hearing, reading, speaking and repeating. Recitation is a lost learning art. Have the courage to speak these catechisms, and the truths will be cemented into your heart and soul. Do it for the sake of your Alpha Omega: Jesus Christ.

Catechism

Question: Where is God?

Answer:
Inside of me, and also everywhere.

Catechism

Question: What is the Church?

Answer:
We are; connected in the right local church where God has placed us.

Catechism

Question: What is my pastor?

Answer:
He is my covering and guardian.
He gives me protection, instruction, direction and correction.
He proves to be an example for me.

Catechism

Question: How do I connect to my pastor?

Answer:
I will consider the result of my pastor's conduct.
I will obey and submit to my pastor in the Lord. I will highly
esteem my pastor in love. I will trust and appreciate my pastor.
I will aspire to bring my pastor joy, not grief.

Catechism

Question: What is prayer?

Answer:
Prayer is conversation: talking with God.

Catechism

Question: What is the Bible?

Answer:
The Word of God, breathed by Him, containing no errors,
and our only objective standard of truth.

Catechism

Question: Where is God's power?

Answer:
Inside of me, and also everywhere.

LEGEND OF THE SPIRIT

- What is the Holy Spirit doing?

- What does the Holy Spirit want?

- What is the Holy Spirit saying?

Revelation 3:13 – "He who has an ear, let him hear what the Spirit says to the churches."

What is the will of the Holy Spirit? He is establishing your heart as His home, where He resides. He loves you, so He enjoys being in you. And He loves receiving your love. He wants you to enjoy His presence within you, to give Him a hug once in awhile and express your love to Him.

- To each one of us He is saying: "I'm here in your heart all the time. Enjoy My presence and love Me as I love you."

What is the will of the Holy Spirit? He is the breath of life in each one of us individually, but also the breath of life in us corporately. That's how the bones with flesh and skin come to life. There is a special way that connected Christians have the life and breath of the Holy Spirit to enliven the group. That is what the Holy Spirit is doing. And He wants every one of us to connect with each other in the local churches that

He has called into being, and designed to be successfully functioning groups.

- To each one of us He is saying, "You are an essential part of your local church. Find your local church, find your place in that church, connect solidly with your fellow Christians in that church, and minister for Jesus!"

What is the will of the Holy Spirit? He raises up leaders for every church to have a pastor. And He does something special: He equips your pastor to do a great job shepherding you; He holds your pastor in His right hand (Revelation 1:16), to give him special help and to hold him accountable. He wants you to put yourself into connecting and relating to your pastor. Do what it takes to receive and enjoy the benefits of his ministry to you.

- The Holy Spirit says, "Your pastor is an under-shepherd to you; place yourself under his ministry and embrace the benefits of being led and shepherded by him. Follow him as he follows Christ!"

What is the will of the Holy Spirit? He draws each one of us to accept Jesus as our Savior and Lord, and then to embrace the truth that we have the righteousness of Jesus Christ, and we are righteous individuals, who are qualified to ask Jesus for anything. He is helping us de-formalize prayer, de-bunk the false and lofty ideas of what prayer is to be, and come down to earth to talk with Him; just to have conversation with Him as our informal and intimate friend. He wants us to talk, talk, talk with Him. He wants to have conversation at any time, in any moment. He wants us to listen and learn to hear Him.

- He is saying, "How's it going? Tell me what's on your mind, what's working for you, what's not; don't be afraid to express your thoughts and feelings to Me; I want to hear you talk, and I want to respond to you."

What is the will of the Holy Spirit? The Holy Spirit is teaching us what the Scripture says and means; He is guiding us into everything by helping us see the applicable Bible verses; He is recalling to our memory whatever Scripture we have read, studied or memorized. He wants us to love the Bible, to handle it carefully and to learn the ways of the Lord from it. That way we can teach all the people who come into the church, seeking how to walk in the ways of the Lord.

- He is saying: I am the Breath (Spirit) of God and I have breathed the Bible for you. Love it, treasure it, read it, study it, and let Me be your guide to the truth."

What is the will of the Holy Spirit? He wants us to experience every aspect of God's nature: His presence (Jehovah) and His power in action (El Shaddai). He is dwelling securely, inside of each one of us, ever ready to give us dynamite power.

- He is saying, "Don't short yourself. Partake of all the power I have for you. Use it in ministry for My kingdom. Be perfected by My power. Embrace Me as I embrace you. I love you and want you as My perfect bride."

ABOUT THE AUTHOR

Reed Tibbetts has served for over twenty-three years as an ordained pastor and teacher, and is currently serving as one of the elders of VLife Church in McKinney, Texas, where he ministers as a prophet and teacher.

An honored and decorated disabled veteran of the Vietnam War, Reed is a graduate of Northwest University of the Assemblies of God. Over the many years he has pursued the goal of handling accurately the word of truth, and has developed a reputation as a guardian of apostolic doctrine (the teachings of the apostles).

Through the years Reed has written and printed many teaching notebooks in the churches he has served, but only recently has he turned to the writing and publishing of books for the greater body of Christ.

Reed lives in Princeton, Texas with his wife of forty-six years. They have three adult children and four grandchildren, all of whom are faithfully serving the Lord in their respective local churches.

AUTHOR CONTACT

Reed has written several other books about the successful Christian life. If you would like to contact him, find out more information, purchase books, or request him to speak, please contact:

Allegro Ministries
470 San Remo
Princeton, TX 75407
yahovah3@gmail.com
214 724-7541

Allegro Ministries is a non-profit corporation, formed by Reed and his family, recognized as a 501(c)(3) by the I.R.S. It exists for the purpose of spreading relevant teachings to the church of the Lord Jesus Christ, so that more and more people can live the brisk and lively Christian walk. If you would like to contribute to the ministry, please send your offerings to the above address, and thank you for your giving.

CPSIA information can be obtained
at www.ICGtesting.com
Printed in the USA
BVOW06s1006250617
487769BV00015B/152/P